# CHOOSE
# GROWTH

# CHOOSE GROWTH

## A WORKBOOK FOR TRANSCENDING TRAUMA, FEAR, AND SELF-DOUBT

SCOTT BARRY KAUFMAN, PhD
& JORDYN H. FEINGOLD, MD

A TarcherPerigee Book

**tarcher**perigee

An imprint of Penguin Random House LLC
penguinrandomhouse.com

Most TarcherPerigee books are available at special quantity discounts for bulk purchase for sales
promotions, premiums, fund-raising, and educational needs. Special books or book excerpts also
can be created to fit specific needs. For details, write: SpecialMarkets@penguinrandomhouse.com.

Library of Congress Cataloging-in-Publication Data
Names: Kaufman, Scott Barry, 1979– author. | Feingold, Jordyn H., author.
Title: Choose growth: a workbook for transcending trauma, fear, and self-doubt /
Scott Barry Kaufman, PhD & Jordyn H. Feingold, MD
Description: New York: TarcherPerigee, [2022]
Identifiers: LCCN 2022017136 (print) | LCCN 2022017137 (ebook) |
ISBN 9780593538630 (trade paperback) | ISBN 9780593538647 (epub)
Subjects: LCSH: Self-actualization (Psychology) | Resilience (Personality trait) |
Adjustment (Psychology) | Change (Psychology)
Classification: LCC BF637.S4 K3948 2022 (print) |
LCC BF637.S4 (ebook) | DDC 158.1—dc23/eng/20220609
LC record available at https://lccn.loc.gov/2022017136
LC ebook record available at https://lccn.loc.gov/2022017137

Printed in the United States of America
1st Printing

Book design by Laura K. Corless

*This book is dedicated to our parents,
for encouraging us to choose growth,
time and time again.*

# CONTENTS

# CONTENTS

## CHAPTER 4

## CHAPTER 5

## CHAPTER 6

# CONTENTS

# INTRODUCTION

> One can choose to go back toward safety or forward toward growth.
> Growth must be chosen again and again;
> fear must be overcome again and again.
> —Abraham Maslow

To exist is a true gift. The mere act of existence is full of possibilities for self-actualization and meaningful contribution. With life you can matter and realize your most unique potentials that only you have. There is no one else in the world who can realize those potentials but *you*.

Human existence is also full of challenges. This is a "given of existence," as the existential psychotherapist Irvin Yalom put it.[1] Indeed, we are living in a time of great change. A global pandemic. An unstable economy. Threats of climate change. Poverty. Inequity. Collapsing governments. War. There are so many reasons to be insecure, uncertain, and apprehensive of the future.

It's not easy being human, and yet here we are. Humans have shown during this time a remarkable capacity to not only survive and adapt, but also to *thrive*. What if these times of great uncertainty can lead to changes that contribute to our greatest sources of self-actualization and transcendence? Let's face it: We're ready for it. We're *craving* it. More people are ready to change their jobs than ever before. According to one survey of U.S. workers, 95 percent said they were considering leaving their jobs due to burnout and a lack of growth opportunities.[2] By September 2021, 4.4 million

Americans took this plunge, in a trend termed the "Great Resignation."[3] Maybe now is that time to try new things. To reprioritize. To *grow*.

This book is about helping all of us transcend—to integrate the many facets of ourselves, in service of realizing the good of society—even under the most challenging of circumstances. We will help you lean in to the growth potential we all have, embrace and cocreate our "new normal," and face future challenges with a renewed sense of vitality, strength, and hope for the future.

The pages of this book are entirely yours: a judgment-free zone to explore your needs and resolve inner conflict and begin to explore how to heal from external conflict as well. It is designed to help build insight and self-understanding to clarify what matters most and how you can choose to nurture those things to ultimately live a richer, more meaningful, and self-actualized life. This book is evidence-based and draws heavily from several areas of psychology, including humanistic psychology, positive psychology, developmental psychology, personality psychology, cognitive science, and neuropsychology.

We're all at different points in our self-actualization journeys, but we've all been through the prolonged uncertainty of a global pandemic that has shaken the very foundations of our lives.

# POST-TRAUMATIC GROWTH

Hardship often prepares an ordinary person
for an extraordinary destiny.
—C. S. Lewis

The human capacity for resilience—bouncing back in the wake of adversity—is often underrated. Resilience researcher George Bonanno found that survivors of trauma tend to exhibit one of three trajectories: chronic symptoms, gradual recovery, or resilience. In almost every analysis he conducted, the resilience trajectory—bouncing back—is the most common pattern found.[4] Bonanno highlights three ingredients that are central to what he terms the "flexibility mindset": optimism or a general belief in a favorable future, confidence in our ability to cope, and a "challenge orientation," or viewing obstacles as challenges, rather than threats.[5] These core ingredients, Bonanno found, are essential for one's ability to bounce back, and, we would add, *spring forward*, after a life-altering event.

Not only is the potential for post-pandemic growth possible, but people are growing right now. According to one large Gallup poll, at the start of the pandemic the percentage of Americans who evaluated their lives well enough to be considered "thriving" was as low as ratings during the Great Recession.[6] However, by June 2021 the percentage of Americans who evaluated their lives well enough to be considered thriving had reached the *highest* levels in more than thirteen years.

We're also finding newfound ways to be grateful. Psychologist Philip Watkins and his colleagues surveyed 511 adult participants from March to May 2020 about their current and future emotions.[7] Even in the thick of the pandemic, more than 56 percent of people reported being very grateful in general, which was 17 percent higher than the responses of any other positive emotion. What's more, 69 percent of respondents expected to feel even *more* grateful in the future. During the pandemic, gratitude was a strong predictor of happiness and significantly predicted the likelihood to help others.

The idea that pain and trauma can be transformed into courage and strength has a long history among humans, as exemplified by everything from art and literature to philosophy and spiritual beliefs. Indeed, the "hero's journey" is a very common narrative throughout literature: The hero explores the world, conquers their inner demons or outer struggles, and comes home changed or strengthened in some victorious way.[8]

The formal scientific study of this fundamentally human transformation boomed in the mid-1990s when psychologists Lawrence Calhoun and Richard Tedeschi coined the term *post-traumatic growth* (PTG). According to these researchers, PTG involves "positive psychological changes experienced as a result of the struggle with traumatic or highly challenging life circumstances."[9] The PTG approach is grounded in existential philosophy and existential-humanistic psychology, approaches to human existence that emphasize the importance of viewing suffering through the lens of the meaning that we ascribe to the event.[10]

Importantly, it's not the traumatic event *itself* that leads to growth, but the cognitive processing and meaning-making during and in the aftermath of the event that has the potential to facilitate significant transformations in our lives. PTG does not deny the discomfort and pain frequently associated with a highly challenging experience, but focuses on how we can grow given that we can't change the past. As the existential psychotherapist Irvin Yalom put it, "Sooner or later [you have] to give up the hope for a better past."[11]

Critically, the event doesn't have to be life-threatening—life-altering is not the same as life-threatening—or cause post-traumatic stress disorder (PTSD). PTG can result from enduring *any* challenging environment that causes a seismic shift in our worldview and assumptions about how we thought the world worked. Critically, what is traumatic to one person may not be considered traumatic to another; indeed, we believe that "trauma" is in the eye of the beholder.

Some common traumatic events found in post-traumatic growth studies include natural disasters, motor vehicle accidents, bereavement, sexual assault, a terminal illness diagnosis, and combat trauma. Over the course of the pandemic, we would add to the list: quarantine and isolation from loved ones; newfound fears of things that previously sustained us most, such as close physical contact; stigma related to infections and infection-control measures; massive cancellations of life events; work and school closures; the total breakdown of barriers among home, work, and school; forced exposure to the virus for those in jobs that didn't allow them to work from home; navigating childcare, homeschooling, and sustaining a living for one's family; rampant death, loss, and despair for both human life and an overall sense of normalcy. The list goes on.

Many of these events are not only life-altering but also *mind-altering* in some significant way, causing us to see the world and ourselves differently. People who report post-traumatic growth tend to report growth in the following areas:[12]

- Greater appreciation of life
- Greater appreciation and strengthening of close relationships
- Greater awareness and utilization of one's personal strengths
- Increased compassion and altruism
- The identification of new possibilities or a purpose in one's life
- Enhanced spiritual development
- Enhanced creative growth

While many of these findings are based on *self-perceived* growth, rather than on the objective behaviors that individuals manifest after trauma,[13] we believe that even just a shift in one's view of the world, capacities, and relations to others can have a profound effect and increase a person's quality of life substantially. This book will help guide you to do just that.

Changes analogous to PTG can also happen in people who have not been exposed to events explicitly considered traumatic and can happen in those who intentionally *choose* suffering.[14] For instance, growth has been found in those who make great sacrifices in their lives to change the world for the better and those who willingly face suffering on their path to mastery. For instance, research has found growth in the aftermath of space travel and solo circumnavigation by sailing.[15] People who choose to endure such challenging environments can be changed in ways that are very much like those changes reported by people who endure unexpected traumatic events. But what about events that happen to us that we do not choose?

For those who have been personally touched and transformed by trauma, post-traumatic growth helps us discover and embrace a belief system we did not previously have.[16] What's more, the development of PTG makes a person more capable of responding more optimally in the face of future trauma.

For those who may consider themselves languishing from pandemic life—feeling stuck, ungrounded, ill at ease, lost, or just plain worn out[17]—we will help you process these experiences and work toward what we call *post-pandemic growth*: using the era of COVID and all that we've been through as a catalyst for living a more examined life, full of transcendent possibility. We believe it is possible to find greater strength, connection, and new possibilities during and in the aftermath of this time.

Of course, growth comes from *many* sources, and we certainly aren't making the claim that growth *requires* suffering.[18] In fact, there is also such a thing as *post-ecstatic growth*, in which we can grow significantly from profoundly positive and inspirational events in our lives.[19] This book will help you spur growth intentionally, regardless of your history of hardships or where you are in your journey.

# WHO ARE WE?

Scott Barry Kaufman is a cognitive scientist and humanistic psychologist exploring the depths of human potential. He is a professor at Columbia University and founder and director of the Center for Human Potential. As a child growing up with learning difficulties, he became fascinated with human intelligence, creativity, and human potential. His fundamental self-narrative for most of his childhood was that he was "disabled," not capable of living a normal life. In ninth grade, with the encouragement of a special-education teacher, he took himself out of special education and signed up for more challenging classes. His entire worldview changed. He realized he loved learning. He loved creating. He loved helping others. Through his podcast, articles, self-actualization coaching, talks, and courses, he applies the latest psychological science to help all kinds of minds reach their full potential and become creative, self-actualized human beings.

In the spring of 2015, Scott's first semester teaching the undergraduate Positive Psychology course at the University of Pennsylvania, Jordyn Feingold, then a college senior, sat on the edge of her seat. Scott could see the wheels spinning as she actively integrated the philosophy, history, and science of positive psychology, the science of human flourishing, into her vision of how she would, one day, practice medicine, and work toward the whole-person well-being of her future patients.

That semester, with Scott's mentorship, Jordyn decided to postpone her medical school application to apply for the Master of Applied Positive Psychology (MAPP) program. She felt called to acquire this foundational knowledge of the good life before going to medical school to learn the ins and outs of disease and body system dysfunction.

Scott and Jordyn stayed in close touch as Jordyn moved to New York City for medical school, and Scott soon followed to teach The Science of Living Well course at Columbia University. They worked together on the evidence-based exercises in Scott's *Transcend: The New Science of Self-Actualization*, released not even one month into COVID lockdowns in April 2020. They also worked together on an online eight-week Transcend course created to help people across the world thrive in the wake of the pandemic.

Jordyn has now graduated from medical school, where she developed an expertise in the brain-gut axis and applications of positive psychology in the treatment of gastro-intestinal disorders, and led transdisciplinary research studying the psychological impact of the pandemic on frontline healthcare workers in New York City—the nation's first epicenter of the pandemic. She cofounded a positive psychology–based peer-support program for medical trainees and works locally and nationally to address burnout and advocate for the well-being of healthcare workers.

In July 2021, Jordyn continued her training as a resident physician in psychiatry, working with patients with complex psychiatric, medical, and neurological disorders, integrating positive psychology and strengths-based approaches to patient care. In these capacities, she appreciates the complex interrelationships among well-being, ill-being, trauma, post-traumatic stress disorder, and its lesser-known cousin PTG, as she works toward catalyzing a paradigm shift in healthcare toward a field she refers to as "positive medicine."

# THIS BOOK

This book is about the *full spectrum* of the human experience, of which suffering is an integral part. We encourage you to lean in to and nurture transformation within yourself as a pathway to healing, self-actualization, and ultimately transcendence.

We have written this book to provide you with critical questions and practices that our students of all ages from all over the world have found to be meaningful drivers of self-discovery and growth, and ones that we are continuously using ourselves as we integrate the science of transcendence into our own lives. Many of the practices are based in evidence and have been tested broadly across diverse people all over the world; where we were not able to find specific practices with an evidence base, we created our own informed by the research, and sincerely hope that they help you.

What is unique about this moment in history is that for the first time in the modern age all humans around the globe have been exposed to a common catastrophe; no one has been completely spared or unchanged. Thus, this book is *human-centered*—we aim to meet you wherever you are, however you've been impacted. Let us embrace what is human about all of us and seize this collective opportunity to grow, personally and collectively. Underneath our tribalism and arbitrary ways of dividing each other, we all have the same basic needs for safety, connection, self-esteem, and love, and we all want to matter, to find meaning, and to live a vital life.

## WHAT THIS BOOK IS *NOT* ABOUT

**This book is *not* about finding "quick fixes" to life's dissatisfaction, languishing, or suffering.** It is about engaging in a deep, lifelong, nonlinear process of learning more about ourselves in relation to our own minds and bodies, others, and the world. Through deliberate reflection looking both inward and outward, we can more adroitly navigate uncertainty, ambivalence, and life's greatest challenges. This book is about developing a steadfast, committed relationship to personal and collective growth.

**This book is *not* a manual filled with secrets for how to "be your best self."** Our goal is not to provide you with an instruction manual or a how-to guide of how to improve your life—no such manual could ever possibly exist. In fact, we would like to break down the notion that there is a single, ideal self that you *should* be striving for. We will help you break free from the "tyrannical shoulds" in your life to find a life that works best *for you*, in your own style, and in such a way that you feel vital and creative.[20] We provide more questions than we do answers, so that you can explore for yourself, and hopefully in conversation with others, the deepest questions of your own humanity. We pose thought-provoking questions, opportunities for reflection, research, and experiments that may help you uncover for yourself what growth might mean *for you*. While we have space within the workbook to jot down notes and reflections, you will likely need an additional notebook or document where you can record responses and continue your reflections.

**This book is *not* a replacement for therapy and mental health treatment.** It is about building insight, experiencing life and ourselves more deliberately, and getting out of "automatic pilot." Something that may reveal itself as part of the growth process is a history of unhealed trauma, reckoning with difficult emotions, or maladaptive thinking or behavioral patterns that have been part of your survival or ability to get through life under very difficult circumstances. Some of you may have grown up in environments akin to battlefields with real violence that have shaped your lived experiences and stress responses today. It may become clear that further exploration of these patterns with a licensed counselor would be beneficial. We highly encourage you to use this book as a starting place for further in-depth exploration with a mental health professional. Critically, whatever comes up, we hope that you will embrace yourself without judgment and simply learn to notice what arises. This doesn't mean that you necessarily *like* what has come up, but you accept it. As the humanistic psychotherapist Carl Rogers put it, "The curious paradox is that when I accept myself just as I am, then I can change."[21]

We wholeheartedly recognize that challenges, stress, and trauma are not evenly distributed across society, and myriad systemic inequities and forms of discrimination make growth more difficult following trauma. Learning how to better manage under these conditions does not absolve us of the responsibility of fighting these disparities at interpersonal, systemic, and societal levels. We hope that these exercises are accessible to everyone and help those who are actively working to dismantle injustice every day to be even better equipped for this task.

Life is not a linear process, but more like the journey of a sailboat through the vast unknown of the sea.[22] We need the sturdiness of our boat to feel safe and secure, but if we're going to grow, we must open our sails and be vulnerable to the inevitable winds and waves of life. Throughout this book, we guide you along this process, starting with securing the base of our boat, and eventually raising our sails and steering through the vast waters.

While we are all undoubtedly in different boats, we are sailing these waters together. The goal is not to stop the waves of life, but to learn how to navigate them with the spirit of exploration, love, purpose, and transcendent wisdom. In this book we will also contemplate what it means to pursue what indigenous wisdom refers to as "community actualization."[23] In our own growth journeys, how can we bring our whole selves to the world in such a way that we raise the tide for everyone and contribute to "cultural perpetuity"?[24]

While you may go through the book in order, you do not have to. We recommend that folks begin with chapter 1, and then you can page through the exercises and pick up with whatever speaks to you in a given moment. This journey is yours. We do ask that you take responsibility for your own psychological safety, and not push yourself to complete an exercise or engage with a topic that you do not feel ready for.

## WHAT DOES IT MEAN TO "CHOOSE GROWTH"?

In this life, there are innumerable decisions that are made for us, and it frankly can be overwhelming to think about just how little ultimate control any of us really has. We cannot choose the families or communities that we are born into, the conditions of our births, or factors as fundamental as the genetic makeup we are endowed with and the resultant predispositions we have to certain personality traits, health, and disease. So, what can we choose?

To a significant degree, we have the choice of how we wish to view the world and ourselves. We can make use of our reflective capacities and commitment to our values to make choices in line with intention, meaning, and the good of the world. We often have much more control over these choices than we may think. However, simply knowing that we may need to make a change is not sufficient for enacting that change. Knowing is not enough. Choosing growth is an action-oriented process that translates self-reflection and personal exploration—where are we now, and where do we want to be?—into behaviors and actions aimed at closing those gaps. We must embrace the inevitable fumbles, the need for course correction, and the knowledge that this is a journey without a definitive destination. We are never done growing. As the humanistic psychoanalyst Karen Horney put it, "It is not only the young

*We are never done growing.*

child who is pliable. All of us retain the capacity to change, even to change in fundamental ways, as long as we live."[25]

Choosing growth today is a way to honor our past, live more deliberately in the present, and nurture the future we hope for. To choose the path of growth is to integrate *all* the various parts of ourselves and uplift the completeness of our human experience. This process involves learning, accepting, and integrating all parts of ourselves, including those dark parts that we may wish to suppress or tuck away. It is when we harmonize these parts of ourselves that we may cultivate greater compassion, connect more deeply with others, extract more meaning and joy from life's lessons, and ultimately contribute to the world in ways that are authentic, gratifying, and synergistic with those around us.

We're all on our unique journey, with different unmet needs that change throughout our lives, but one thing is certain: We can't do it alone. We must open the sail and engage with the world to grow. We must choose growth!

## CHAPTER 1

# Anchor Yourself

Before setting sail, let's experience what it feels like to get on the boat and anchor ourselves. Throughout this chapter, we will set you up for a smooth ride through the sometimes choppy and often unpredictable waters of life and the growth process. We will familiarize you with the features of your proverbial sailboat, your vessel throughout this growth journey; introduce you to those who may be on this ride with you; prepare you for the whole-body nature of this experience; and help you to secure the base of your boat. Let's begin.

## WHAT DO YOU NEED?

Every human on the planet has fundamental needs that make us far more similar than we are different from one another. You have likely heard of the renowned "Maslow's Hierarchy of Needs," the pyramid structure attributed to Abraham Maslow, which posits that humans are motivated by increasingly "higher" levels of needs. As it's been interpreted and taught in psychology courses and pop psychology, the more basic needs—physical health, safety, belonging, and esteem—must be satisfied to a certain degree before we can fully self-actualize, becoming all that we can become.[1]

The truth is, though, as Scott details in his book *Transcend: The New Science of Self-Actualization*, Maslow never actually created a pyramid to represent his hierarchy of needs.[2] Whereas the pyramid shape implies we must ascend some metaphorical mountain until we complete each step, unlock the next level of possibility, and never look back, this is an unfortunate misrepresentation of the human condition. Maslow emphasized that we are in a constant state of maturation, and that growth is often a two-steps-forward, one-step-back phenomenon. Evolving in our human condition is not any one destination we are moving toward; it is an *experience*.

To guide us through our growth experience, Scott developed a flexible and functional new metaphor, *the sailboat*, to help us all conceptualize how the fundamental human needs really operate.

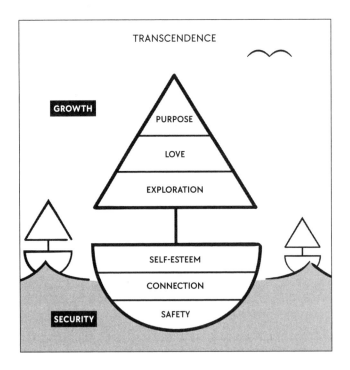

With holes in our boat, we can't go anywhere. When we are living in unsafe conditions, experiencing profound loneliness, or have poor perceptions of ourselves and our own abilities, our energy is often spent simply trying to stay afloat, plugging up the holes and keeping the water out to avoid disaster. Under more favorable conditions, the security needs of safety, connection, and self-esteem operate together to bring our lives stability and bolster us against the harsh waters of life.

But we don't stop there. Also essential to our human condition is *growth*, becoming all that we can become, what Maslow described as being "fully human." To grow, we can't just have a stable base, which is concerned primarily with defense and protection, but we must open our sails with vulnerability to life's winds and waves. Our sail enables us to be curious, open to understanding new truths about the world, to expand ourselves and discover new possibilities for our lives. The growth needs of exploration, love, and purpose function to help us revel in the beauty and goodness in the world and find our own place within it. In this "being realm of human existence," we see the world on its own terms, not only to the extent to which the world and people can satisfy our deficiencies.

As we'll uncover throughout the practices in the workbook, as we fortify our sailboat, it's not just about the level we reach or how large our sail is, but the integration and harmony we have within our boat, with ourselves, with our crewmates, and with the vast water around us. *Transcendence*, which rests on a secure foundation of both security and growth, allows us to attain wisdom and a sense of connectedness with the rest of humanity. Here's the catch, though: We can't seek transcendence directly. Rather, transcendent experiences come along for the ride of working on ourselves and engaging deeply with the world around us.

Let's begin to reflect on how our own proverbial boats have withstood the waves of our lives, and where we may have room for reengineering.

## PRACTICE

1. Spend some time quietly reflecting on the above passage and the sailboat image in the context of your own life. Consider the following questions about your own needs.

SECURITY
- In what ways do I feel safe and secure in my life right now?
- In what ways does my safety feel challenged?

- How is the general quality of my connections with other people?
- What does my own internal dialogue or inner voice sound like?
- Are there any areas in my life in which I feel like I'm just barely getting by?
- How am I generally feeling about myself these days?

GROWTH
- How am I generally feeling about the future?
- What am I excited about right now?
- What parts of myself and what parts of life am I most interested in exploring?
- What is bringing me a sense of meaning in my life?
- What types of things do I want to give my whole self to?
- In what ways do I feel whole?
- What makes me feel fully alive and vital?

2. Use the space below to fill in what your own sailboat looks like right now. Are there holes in the base of your boat? Your sail? What areas of your boat require your greatest attention right now to help you meet your needs?

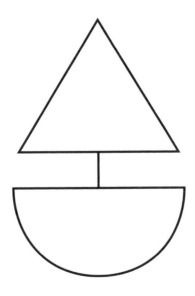

3. Based on the state of your sailboat, what have you discovered already about your needs and how they may be currently met or challenged? What is at least one intention you have for the rest of this journey?

# WHO'S IN YOUR BOAT?

Now that we've taken stock of the state of our boats, let's think about who will be joining us along the ride. While this is designed to be a deeply personal adventure, it is not a solo expedition. Our pursuit of growth is a deeply *interpersonal* process, and research shows that having someone close such as a friend, romantic partner, or colleague who affirms our growth ideals enhances our ability to reach our goals and contributes to greater life satisfaction and psychological health.[3]

We hope that you will choose to share some of the insights and revelations that you have about yourself and how you operate in the world with other people—friends, family members, partners, coworkers, or even a therapist or coach. Perhaps you will be moved to bring a particular topic to a family meal, your team at work, or your special someone. Maybe you'll engage a book club or reading group for accountability and support. Additionally, as we move into deeper waters, there may be times when we will feel out of our depths. Let's prepare for inevitable discomfort by thinking through who we might call upon to throw us a life vest so that we may, more safely, move into the unknown waters head-on.

## PRACTICE

### 1. Identify your crew.

1. Who in your life comprises your "crew," or the folks you would want in your sailboat with you, to help support your growth and hold you accountable on the journey ahead? (These folks can include anyone who you share your life with,

alive or dead, humans or animals, who you can engage with literally or spiritually, through writing, journaling, or prayer.)

2. Who might you call in your "SOS" moments, or ask for help or an open ear when the going gets tough, and when unpleasant sensations, thoughts, or emotions might start to feel overwhelming?

3. Who might you engage with when you experience revelations, beauty, or the "aha" moments ahead? Is there anyone in your life who you love sharing positive news with, who helps you capitalize on the good stuff that happens to you?

## 2. Self check-in.

Take a moment to pause here and reflect on how challenging or simple this task was for you. Where do you find yourself?

| I can't think of a single person to bring with me on this journey. I am alone in this world. | I have people in my life but no one I feel close enough to share this process with. | I am inundated with robust connections in my life, I don't know if there will be room on my sailboat for my giant crew! |
| --- | --- | --- |

Some readers may identify just how many rich connections they have to other human beings. These people ought to consider themselves very blessed, as human connection is one of the greatest gifts we can have in our lives, and as we'll explore in the next chapter, one of the greatest predictors of well-being, health, and life satisfaction.

Some of us may realize that although we have plenty of people in our lives, we can't really identify those who we would genuinely want—or feel comfortable—to share our most intimate struggles or quest for self-knowledge with. We can certainly experience loneliness even in the company of others. This awareness is important and may signal the presence of low-quality connections and an opportunity to work on these. If this is the case, consider revisiting this practice after you complete the practices in chapter 2. Still, not an insignificant number of us may genuinely be thinking, "I have no one to share these experiences with," or, "I am alone in this world, there's really no one." If this is the case, spend a moment reflecting:

- How have I gotten here to this place of isolation? Is this by my choice, or the culmination of a series of choices I've made, or perhaps a result of unfortunate circumstances, such as loss of life of loved ones, or other reasons?
- How is this life of solitude working out for me? Would this be my preference if I could choose?

Given the ultimate importance of relationships in our lives and the pervasiveness of loneliness in our world, we implore you to explore the following:

- Are there connections that I have been neglecting, intentionally or not, with whom I might rekindle? Is there anyone to whom I might owe a phone call?
- What other actions might I take to put myself out there and reengage with people in more deliberate ways?

### 3. Call on your crew, wisely.

Keep your crewmates top of mind as you proceed through the workbook; consider reaching out to them to reflect, laugh, or seek support. Many of us may hold back from asking for support when we need it because we don't wish to be a burden to others. However, this impulse is often misled, as research shows that *providing* support may lead to even greater psychological benefits than receiving it.[4] Indeed, helping others helps oneself; by reaching out and asking for help, we can give others the gift of giving.

Think back to the last time someone asked you for help or sought your advice or counsel on a personal matter.

- How did it feel to be recruited to help someone in need? What was the experience like for you?
- Did you feel bothered in any way? If so, what bothered you?
  *If so, perhaps you were asked at an inconvenient time, or someone made demands of you that you were unable to fulfill. Maybe your counsel was ignored or misinterpreted, or someone asked to help with something that you had little personal experience with or interest in. Whatever you disliked*

*about your own giving experience, remember these pitfalls when asking for help from others.*

- What felt good about helping this person? How might helping have reinforced your own sense of mastery?

Reflecting on your own giving experience, think about how you might ask others for help in ways that will be most energizing for them.

# MIND, MEET BODY

Growth isn't just a mental process that exists above our necks; it is a whole-person experience demanding that we attune to our bodies, in relationship with other minds and bodies around us. This idea of mind-body integration, or *holism*, was central to the ancient wisdom of philosophers Plato and Aristotle, as well as Hippocrates (460–370 BCE), who is widely known for touting physical activity as a remedy for psychological distress: "If you're in a bad mood, go for a walk. If you're still in a bad mood, go for another walk."

However, this ethos largely fell out of fashion in the seventeenth century, when French philosopher René Descartes proposed the theory of *dualism*—that the mind and body are distinct and separate entities—and this artificial separation still largely dominates modern medical practice today. As a result, many of us, especially in the Western world, grossly misunderstand how we can learn from the wisdom of our bodies and capitalize on our mind-body synergy to pursue greater health and well-being.

The Polyvagal theory proposed by Dr. Stephen Porges states that humans and other social mammals operate in three distinct physiological-mental states, *fight-or-flight*, *freeze*, and *social engagement*.[5] Transitions among them are mediated by the activity of two long nerves in our body, collectively known as the vagus nerve, that connects our brainstem to our internal organs, including our facial and throat muscles, pharynx, larynx, esophagus, stomach, intestines, heart, and lungs. Let's explore what goes on inside of us in each state.

1. **Fight-or-flight.** In this state, a part of our nervous system known as the sympathetic nervous system releases neurohormones like adrenaline, raises our blood pressure and heart rate, mobilizes our body's fuel stores for immediate use, dilates our airways to optimize oxygen delivery to our vital organs, and turns off digestion and other functions not immediately related to our survival (including our ability to relate to others). These physical changes are often accompanied by feelings like anger, frustration, irritation, and even rage as we move toward a threatening stimulus (to "fight"), or worry, anxiety, fear, and panic as we run away (take "flight"). Although this ancient defense evolved to keep us alive in times of grave danger, today it is more often triggered by even innocuous stressors of daily life: an overwhelming to-do list, an argument with our spouse, or that dirty dish that has been sitting in our sink for three days.

2. **Freeze.** This state evolved to facilitate conserving energy and reducing our metabolic demands in times of true crisis. In this mode, one portion of the vagus nerve, the dorsal vagus nerve, stimulates fuel storage and lowers our heart rate, blood pressure, body temperature, and muscle tone (think fainting or even hibernation). Sexual functioning and social behaviors are reduced, and we may feel helpless, trapped, and depressed. The freeze state may be associated with suicidal thoughts and dissociation (feeling "outside" of ourselves). Because of these ancient connections between our brains and our bodies, when we spend too much time immobilized (think sitting on the couch, vegging out, without adequate physical activity), our brains may perceive us to be in the "freeze" state and shut down, muddying our ability to think and hijacking our emotions, resulting in low mood.

3. **Social engagement.** This is the most recent state to evolve and is unique to social mammals (sorry, reptile and amphibian friends), defined by feelings of safety, connection, and awareness of the environment. Activation of a distinct portion of the

vagus nerve, the ventral vagus, leads to enhanced digestion, optimal immune functioning, circulation of blood to nonvital organs including our skin and limbs, and the release of chemicals like oxytocin, which fosters social bonds and connection. In this state, we may feel present, at ease, and experience positive, prosocial emotions.

What's fascinating about this theory is the idea that our bodies, not our conscious minds, sense and reflexively distinguish internal and external features that are safe, dangerous, or life threatening, a phenomenon Porges calls *neuroception*.[6] Because our thinking brains are not directly involved in the reflex, we may be wildly inaccurate in our estimation of threat (explaining why that dirty dish can make us feel the same way our ancestors did when they saw a saber-toothed tiger). Our vagus nerve doesn't know (or care) if we are really in danger or if only our egos are.[7]

Alas, because the state we are in can so vastly alter our emotions, moods, and experiences with the world—including the way we perceive information and engage with others—how might we bring greater awareness to our bodies, and learn to modify and support shifts in our physiology to unlock desired shifts within our minds?

# PRACTICE

## 1. Identify what each state means for you.

Complete the table on the following page to tap into what each state feels like in your mind and body. Consider which state you are in right now, and how even just reflecting on the other states feels in your body as you complete the practice.

| | FIGHT-OR-FLIGHT | FREEZE | SOCIAL ENGAGEMENT |
|---|---|---|---|
| What are some words I associate with each of these states, based on my own experiences? | E.g., *stress, overwhelm, anger* | E.g., *shut down, numb, alone, hopeless* | E.g., *alive, joyful, at ease* |
| What does this state feel like in my body? | E.g., *fast heart rate, trouble breathing, feeling suffocated* | E.g., *immobile, stuck, foggy, constricted* | E.g., *connected, open, warm* |
| Where does my mind go when I am in this state? | E.g., *focus on eliminating the threat, difficulty focusing on my goals, angry thoughts* | E.g., *rumination, blank mind, dark thoughts* | E.g., *able to follow my interests, focus and pay attention* |

## 2. Identify your cues.

Using the checklists on the next page, fill out as many cues as you can think of that prompt you into each state. You may think of cues as the triggers for the fight-or-flight and freeze states, for example, a recent argument with your boss or spouse, the death or illness of a loved one, sitting in traffic, and so on. Cues for the social engagement state might include getting a massage, having coffee with a friend, reading, practicing yoga, moving your body physically, or even sex!

| FIGHT-OR-FLIGHT | FREEZE | SOCIAL ENGAGEMENT |
|---|---|---|
| *Cues* | *Cues* | *Cues* |
| ❑ _____ | ❑ _____ | ❑ _____ |
| ❑ _____ | ❑ _____ | ❑ _____ |
| ❑ _____ | ❑ _____ | ❑ _____ |
| ❑ _____ | ❑ _____ | ❑ _____ |
| ❑ _____ | ❑ _____ | ❑ _____ |
| ❑ _____ | ❑ _____ | ❑ _____ |
| ❑ _____ | ❑ _____ | ❑ _____ |
| ❑ _____ | ❑ _____ | ❑ _____ |
| ❑ _____ | ❑ _____ | ❑ _____ |

### 3. Pay attention to what state you're in, in real time.

As you go about engaging with the world, and certainly through the practices throughout the workbook, bring your awareness to which state you are in, and how this state shapes your bodily sensations, thoughts, feelings, and behaviors. Practice deliberately trying out one of your social engagement cues to spark your body's transition into a calmer, more open state of being. You may also try any of the following practices to directly stimulate your ventral vagal nerve to promote transition into the social engagement state:

- **Cool off.** Cooling the body with a cold shower (even for just a few seconds) or a splash of cold water on the face can activate the vagus nerve and reduce signals from the fight-or-flight system.
- **Engage in slow, deep, diaphragmatic breathing.** The exhalation portion of our breath directly stimulates the vagus nerve as it courses through our diaphragm, sending physiologic signals of calm through our bodies. Take several deep breaths, in through your nose and out through your mouth for at least three seconds each, and progressively increase the length of your breath (especially the exhale)!

- **Hum or sing.** When we vocalize (or even gargle liquid), we can directly stimulate the vagus nerve on its path down the body through the throat. Many people reflexively hum or sing in times of stress to self-soothe; try it for yourself.
- **Laugh.** Aside from the obvious benefits of laughter to bring about a more positive mood, the body's experience of laughter literally stimulates our vagus nerve to allow calm to wash over the body.
- **Move.** Physical activity is one of the best things we can do for our bodies and minds. When we move, we stimulate a factor in our brains that is like mood-enhancing fertilizer for our brain cells. We also signal to our bodies that it is time to be alert, resulting in enhanced cognition and problem-solving ability. Our human ancestors did evolve to walk many miles every day. What's even cooler is that when we simply give ourselves credit for the physical tasks that we're already doing, like housework, we can elicit corresponding physiologic benefits without any actual changes in our activity level![8] Give yourself credit for every stair you climb and stroll you take.
- **Meditate.** Meditation is associated with vast benefits for our vagal tone and helping to override our body's reflex into fight-or-flight toward the social engagement state.
- **"Earth" yourself.** If you are able, spend some time allowing your bare feet to meet a natural surface such as grass, sand, dirt, or water. The energy transfer between the Earth and our bodies is associated with many physical and psychological benefits, including enhanced well-being, sleep, energy levels, wound healing, and reduced pain and inflammation.[9]

# FACE YOUR FEARS

Courage is not the absence of fear, but the triumph over it.
—Nelson Mandela

Fear is a profoundly powerful driver of our behavior. One fear that has been front and center for many of us is the fear of the unknown, or the fear caused by the absence of reliable information and sustained uncertainty. There are few things more fear- and anxiety-provoking than the unknown, especially for individuals whose early lives have been fraught with violence, abuse, or neglect, and as a result have developed highly sensitive, hypervigilant, and generalized fear-response systems.

Consistently operating out of fear (*i.e.*, in the fight-or-flight or freeze state) can bring out the worst in us—mentally and physically. Living in fear puts us in a state of perpetual self-defense, attempting to preserve our security and survival often at the expense of openness to connection, love, and growth. To get out of preservation mode, we may need to rethink certain automatic behaviors that reinforce the fears that are not serving us.

Child development psychologists Nathan Fox and Jack Shonkoff note that "fears are not just passively forgotten over time; they must be actively unlearned."[10] Similarly, Steven Maier and Martin Seligman concluded recently that they had their famous theory of "learned helplessness" completely backward: Passivity and lack of control is a default response in animals, an automatic reaction to prolonged adversity.[11] People must actively *unlearn* helplessness and learn to perceive that we can control and harness the unpredictability in our environments.

Even those who have come from childhoods fraught with adversity are capable of extraordinary resilience and can regain a sense of control over their automatic fear responses.[12] As Abraham Maslow noted, one way of overcoming our anxieties is to render our deepest fears "familiar, predictable, manageable, controllable . . . to know them and understand them."[13]

This practice is about doing just that: getting acquainted with some of the psychological fears that are operating under the surface of our consciousness and understand how these fears manifest in our bodies and minds. Indeed, the fear itself is often far worse than reality; even when our fears do materialize, they may be different in texture than we imagined them to be, and we may manifest a remarkable ability to respond and adapt in ways we could not have accounted for.

This exercise is not about becoming numb to real threats to our safety in daily life, or in necessarily targeting specific phobias.* Instead, it's about gaining greater agency over some of the psychological fears that may be holding us back and keeping us in defensive, self-preservation mode.

## PRACTICE

### 1. Reflect on past fear.

Find a comfortable, quiet place where you can safely close your eyes for a few moments of reflection. With closed or downcast eyes, reflect upon a fear that you experienced in the past that you overcame. This may be a fear from your childhood or earlier in your life or more recently. This does not have to be a particularly profound fear, just something that previously made you uncomfortable, that you perhaps sought to avoid, but eventually faced and overcame. Reflect on the following:

- What was the fear?
- Before I faced the fear, what did the fear, or thoughts about this fear, feel like in my body?
- Did I avoid reminders of the fear? If so, how?
- How did I eventually face the fear? What did it take? Did anyone help me?

---

* Fears are not the same thing as phobias. Fears are common reactions to events or objects in our lives; phobias are clinical phenomena that interfere with functioning; they're like fears on steroids. Phobias are some of the most common psychiatric disorders people experience, categorized in the DSM-5 as anxiety disorders. Common phobias include heights (acrophobia), spiders (arachnophobia), elevators or tight spaces (claustrophobia), and open, crowded spaces, often associated with panic attacks (agoraphobia). The most successful treatment for specific phobias includes a form of cognitive behavioral therapy (CBT) known as exposure and response prevention therapy, where patients are gradually exposed to higher "doses" of a fear-inducing stimulus until the phobia is extinguished.

Now sit with this scenario for a moment. Really hold the space to reflect on how you confronted the fear. Bask in this and don't shy away from giving yourself a little credit and holding gratitude for whoever may have helped you.

Next, as you think about a current fear that you might be experiencing, remember, you have faced a fear before; you can do it again!

## 2. Connect with a current fear.

When you are ready, recall a fear that you are experiencing now that may be causing unwanted distress. This can be something concrete (*e.g.*, having a difficult conversation) or perhaps something a bit less tangible (*e.g.*, a general sense of anxiety about work or social events). Whatever fear you focus on, consider whether this may represent a deeper psychological fear. To help with this, review the Psychological Fears Scale, and see if your fear aligns with any or multiple of these psychological fears. As you explore potential fear, practice withholding any self-judgment. In fact, this scale captures fears that are universal parts of the human experience.

PSYCHOLOGICAL FEARS SCALE[14]

*Fear of Failure*

❑ I am afraid of failing in somewhat difficult situations when a lot depends on me.

❑ I feel uneasy doing something if I am not sure of succeeding.

❑ If I do not understand a problem immediately, I start to feel anxious.

*Fear of Rejection*

❑ When I get to know new people, I often fear being rejected by them.

❑ Being given the cold shoulder when approaching strangers makes me feel insecure.

❑ Being rejected is a big deal for me.

*Fear of Losing Control*

❑ I become scared when I lose control over things.

❑ I start worrying instantly when I notice that I don't have an impact on some things.

❑ The idea of not having any control in a situation frightens me.

### Fear of Losing Emotional Contact

❏  I am absolutely devastated if a good friend breaks off contact with me.

❏  I become agitated when I lose emotional contact with my loved ones.

❏  If a close friend blows me off, I become anxious about our relationship.

### Fear of Losing Reputation

❏  I would be very worried if my good reputation was in danger.

❏  I'm very keen on an undamaged reputation.

*(Note: You can of course complete this exercise multiple times with different fears, so try to select one at a time; feel free to skip any steps that feel unhelpful to you.)*

- What is it that I am afraid of? (Get specific!)
- Why is this so scary to me? What psychological fears may be underlying this situation?
- What sensations do I experience in my body when I think about this fear?
- What would facing this fear head-on look like?
  - What internal conditions (*e.g.,* my personal strengths, attitudes, preparation) might help me face this fear?
  - What external factors (*e.g.,* help from others, a specific time or place) might help me face this fear?
- If this fear were to come to fruition, what is the worst possible outcome?
  - How likely do you think it is for the worst possible outcome to happen? (0 to 100 percent)

Pause here for a self-check. *How am I feeling now? Is there any value in taking a few deep, diaphragmatic breaths to ease my body? Do I feel the need to take a walk or do some jumping jacks to discharge some energy or clear my head with music or other forms of distraction? How can I give myself what I need in this moment, without judgment?*

When you are ready, return to the prompts.

- Are there any potentially favorable outcomes of this fear unfolding and having to face my fear?
- In what ways might I grow by facing this fear? What might I learn?

Self-check: If, at this stage, facing your fear feels completely insurmountable and anxiety-provoking, just sit with that. Consider confronting a "less scary" fear first for practice.

## 3. Rehearse it!

When you are ready, begin to rehearse facing your fear. This does not mean that you are going to, this minute, conquer or extinguish a fear that has been gnawing at you for months or years; it does mean beginning to imagine the process unfolding. Imagine facing the fear. Repeat this process of mental rehearsal several times, noticing how the physical sensations in your body change with each repetition.

- What happens in my body as I rehearse facing my fear?

Continue the mental rehearsal until you are confident that you can face this fear (or begin to dip your toe in the water of facing this fear). Remember: There will always be variables that arise that we cannot possibly account for. This is part of the adventure.

## 4. Face it!

When you attempt to face this fear, reflect on how it went:

- What went well?
- What might I do differently next time?
- What, if anything, is still unresolved?
- Is there anyone I can call on to help?

It can be very helpful to become aware of those moments when we are automatically operating from a place of fear, and when our fears get in the way of pursuing or achieving our goals. Self-awareness is a crucial first step toward stepping out of behavioral patterns that may no longer serve our growth.

# SECURE YOUR ATTACHMENT

Much of our perceptions of our safety and security in the world, and, more narrowly, our evaluations of our own goodness and worth, begin to develop in our infancy in relation to our caregivers, well before we are even consciously aware of our surroundings. Attachment theory, pioneered by British psychologist John Bowlby and Canadian developmental psychologist Mary Ainsworth, posits that distinct attachment patterns, or ways of behaving in the caregiver-infant relationship, may predict the ways in which we behave in our adult relationships and, ultimately, view ourselves in relation to the world.

Of course, infants eventually grow into adults, and our adult attachment style plays a role in the stability and growth of our adult relationships. Psychologists have identified two main adult attachment dimensions: anxious and avoidant, both of which lie on a continuum.[15]

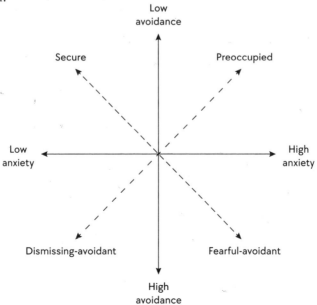

The *anxiety* dimension (horizontal axis) reflects concerns about being rejected or abandoned and is related to how we believe others will be there for us in times of need. The *avoidance* dimension (the vertical axis) reflects how we regulate our emotions during times of stress—do we reach out to others for safety, or tend to pull back or withdraw from them? Depending on our placement on both dimensions, we will end up in one of four quadrants: secure, preoccupied, fearful-avoidant, or dismissing-avoidant.

Note that, interestingly, the *secure attachment* style is simply a product of being low on both the anxiety and avoidant spectra; and let us emphasize that these are both SPECTRA! Securely attached individuals tend to feel more emotional safety in their relationships, are more likely to believe that others are there for them in times of need, and are more likely to reach out to others when they feel unsafe, rather than retreat and withdraw into themselves. However, research suggests that there is truly no such thing as a *completely* securely attached person—all of us have a little bit of anxiety and avoidance in our relationships, especially during times of stress.

The research also suggests that the relationship between our childhood and adult attachment styles is not very strong.[16] What's reassuring about this is that our working models can very much change over time—especially in the presence of a partner who is sensitive to our main attachment triggers—and none of us are destined to live out the insecure patterns that we may have developed from childhoods of overindulgence, insensitive parenting, or even neglect that we may have experienced.[17]

*It all starts with awareness.*

It all starts with awareness: The more aware we are that these patterns exist, the more we can gain insight and work to understand our own behaviors and needs. This will significantly help us modify maladaptive behaviors, express our needs to others, and understand the needs and behaviors of others, so that we may feel safe in and genuinely flourish in our relationships.

## PRACTICE

### 1. Build insight.

Spend some time honestly reflecting on the relationships you have in your life in general, including family relationships, romantic relationships, friendships, and workplace relationships. Don't just think about how you relate to others during the good times and smooth sailing; also consider how you engage with others and what you expect of others during stressful or challenging times. (Remember the start of the pandemic? Consider how you reacted when you were likely forced to drastically change the way you interacted with others.)

Consider: What do you suspect is your dominant attachment style (secure, preoccupied, fearful-avoidant, or dismissing-avoidant)? As a rough guide to which quadrant you might lie on in the attachment spectra, read the following statements, thinking about whether each statement sounds "very much like me," "not at all like me," or somewhere in between:

A. It is easy for me to become emotionally close to others. I am comfortable depending on them and having them depend on me. I don't worry about being alone or having others not accept me. (*Secure*)

B. I want to be completely emotionally intimate with others, but I often find that others are reluctant to get as close as I would like. I am uncomfortable being without close relationships, but I sometimes worry that others don't value me as much as I value them. (*Preoccupied*)

C. I am uncomfortable getting close to others. I want emotionally close relationships, but I find it difficult to trust others completely or to depend on them. I worry that I will be hurt if I allow myself to become too close to others. (*Fearful-avoidant*)

D. I am comfortable without close emotional relationships. It is very important to me to feel independent and self-sufficient, and I prefer not to depend on others or have others depend on me. (*Dismissing-avoidant*)

- What are some of the behaviors and thoughts that I have in my relationships that indicate to me that this is my dominant style?
- How might these thoughts and behaviors serve me in my relationship(s)?
- How might these thoughts and behaviors cause me distress or lead to conflict with others?
- When I think about the people whom I'm closest to in this world, what do I suspect their attachment styles to be? How do I know?

## 2. Practice honesty and vulnerability with yourself and others.

Be mindful of how anxious and avoidant tendencies come up in real time within your relationships. Catch yourself having any version of the following thoughts:

- "Why should I bother reaching out to others? No one is really there for me anyway."
- "I'm going to be alone forever anyway, why even put myself out there?"
- "No one will ever understand how I feel, it's too exhausting to even explain myself."
- "If I didn't reach out to her, she would never have reached out to me . . ."
- "When he does things without me, it signals that he doesn't need me."

When you experience any of these thoughts (or similar ones), or find yourself withdrawing from others or instigating conflict, take note of what's happening. Instead of judging yourself for these thoughts or feelings, blaming your partner for misunderstanding you, or overvaluing these ideas, think about steps you might take to challenge these tendencies toward anxiety and avoidance. Consider: *How might I lean in to this relationship instead of withdrawing out of fear of being abandoned? How might I ask for help instead of assuming it's not there for me? How might I advocate for what I need in a relationship?*

## 3. Commit to change (and recommit, and recommit . . .).

If the goal is to embody a more secure attachment style, we can start by recognizing that this transformation will not happen overnight. Play and replay step 2 above in your relationships in real time and think about the most securely attached person you know. How might they behave in a situation we find ourselves in that is particularly challenging?

~~~~~~~~~~~~~~~~~~~~~~~~~~~~~~~~~~~~~~~~~~~~~~~~~~~~~~~~~~

*For existing partners who are ready to dive into vulnerability right away, see the "Grow Together" practice in the next chapter.*

*If facing your own attachment style brings about an overwhelming sense of fear or discomfort, consider applying this to "Face Your Fears" in this chapter, or "Expand Your Comfort Zone" in chapter 4.*

## CHAPTER 2

# Connect

Those around us, in our corner,
shape who we are more than nearly any other factor.
Behaviors, emotions, and even values are contagious.
If something infiltrates our group, it becomes part of us as well.
—Steve Magness, high-performance expert, on Twitter,
September 7, 2021

The power of human connection—the need to belong, to be accepted, and to have intimate, mutual relationships with at least a few people—is undeniable. One of the most powerful evolutionary survival mechanisms we have had to flourish as a species is to be part of a community or tribe, to share resources, responsibilities, work, child-rearing, and joy among a collective. Nearly a century of research supports the need for connection and positive relationships as the single most important factor for well-being and life satisfaction, and its critical role in health and longevity.[1]

Since we are inherently social creatures, being on the edge of the social perimeter is, frankly, a precarious position.[2] Given the conditions of our hunter-gatherer past on the savannah, lone wolves of our ancestral world could simply not bear the unforgiving conditions alone, and thus, the need to belong, to be liked and accepted, as well as the need for intimacy, mutuality, and relatedness, came to have a central role in our human psyche. Consequently, as the threat-detecting creatures we are, modern humans have developed exquisitely sensitive "social protection systems" to keep us on our toes to socially undesirable conditions, such as exclusion or ostracism.[3]

Social psychologist John Cacioppo has found that social pain, or the perception of low belonging in a community, is indistinguishable from physical pain, with severe consequences on the functioning of the whole person. An ostracized human brain enters a "self-preservation state" (our freeze mode) that brings with it a slew of unwanted effects, including the development of depressive disorders, the adoption of avoidance behaviors and social isolation, the development of malignant narcissism, and even "micro-awakenings" and sleep disruption in the middle of the night as our brains remain on high alert for threats.[4]

In today's world, where, paradoxically, social connection is more accessible than ever before through the ubiquity of social media, exclusion, ostracism, and upward comparison are also increasingly visible. In the United States, suicide rates have increased 25 percent since 1999, with the rates among fifteen- to twenty-four-year-olds rising steadily since 2007.[5] Since 2005, there have been more mass-shooting incidents and deaths than there were in the previous twenty-three years combined.[6]

As with all our needs, various factors, including our genes, environments, and early childhood experiences, lead to a great deal of heterogeneity in the population regarding how much connection each of us requires. Reflect on the following statements to understand where you fall in the two needs that comprise the need for connection: belonging and intimacy.

| NEED FOR BELONGING[7] | NEED FOR INTIMACY[8] |
|---|---|
| ❑ I try hard not to do things that will make other people avoid or reject me. | ❑ I have a close, intimate relationship with someone. |
| ❑ I need to feel that there are people I can turn to in times of need. | ❑ I like to fully immerse myself in a relationship. |
| ❑ I want other people to accept me. | ❑ I want to be able to share all the good and negative emotions in a relationship. |
| ❑ I do not like being alone. | ❑ I don't like to be separated from the people I really care about. |

| NEED FOR BELONGING | NEED FOR INTIMACY |
|---|---|
| ❏ It bothers me a great deal when I am not included in other people's plans.<br><br>❏ My feelings are easily hurt when I feel that others do not accept me.<br><br>❏ I have a strong need to belong. | ❏ My thoughts often revolve around my loved ones.<br><br>❏ Sometimes I feel a deep connection and complete unity with another.<br><br>❏ I don't keep any secrets from the people I love. |

As we read through these statements, the critical metric is not how much we agree or disagree with them, but rather the distance between our need for belonging and the degree to which this need is currently met in our daily lives.[9]

Of course, the advent of the COVID-19 pandemic has uniquely and indiscriminately impacted our ability to connect with others and satisfy our needs for connection, belonging, and intimacy. With social distancing guidelines implemented to curtail the spread of the virus, our immediate safety and survival has been placed at odds with our deep-seated need for connection (at least, in-person connection): hugging, holding hands, sharing a meal. The World Health Organization (WHO) has acknowledged this conundrum by announcing early in the pandemic that the term *physical distancing* was more suitable to capture the distancing guidelines intended to slow the disease, emphasizing that individuals should remain physically, but not socially, distant from others.[10]

While physical distancing and social isolation are not synonymous, as physical distancing still enables virtual, telephonic, and within-household interaction, for many people, the protracted course of the pandemic has contributed to chronic loneliness. Research shows that the quality and quantity of relationships folks had at the start of the pandemic were great predictors of how individuals fared adjusting to life with COVID-19. Other factors such as pre-existing mental health conditions, the presence of a chronic illness, and age impacted the level of loneliness people felt during the pandemic, often with mixed and nuanced effects.[11] Given the heterogeneity of social experiences throughout these last few years, we implore you to think about the following for yourself:

- How have I shown up in my relationships throughout the various ebbs and flows of pandemic life?
- How might I have avoided showing up in some relationships?
  - How have these behaviors served me? How have they been potentially harmful?
- When have I felt the loneliest?
- When have I felt the most connected?
- How has my social media use shaped the ways in which I've felt connected to others?
  - How does passively scrolling on various platforms tend to make me feel?
  - How does actively posting and engaging with my community tend to make me feel?
- How have my personality characteristics helped me to thrive socially?
- How have my personality characteristics made it hard for me to thrive socially?
- In what ways has my community contracted or expanded recently?
- Is there anyone in my life to whom I owe a phone call right now?
- Is there anyone in my life with whom I'm holding a grudge, or harboring resentment?

As we move through life and aim to cultivate growth, one of the most high-yield investments we can make is a steadfast commitment to our relationships. The people we surround ourselves with, physically, virtually, emotionally, and spiritually, shape our realities in profound ways. Robust bodies of research show that happiness, health, and well-being are not just functions of our individual experience, but rather are properties of the groups we are a part of.[12] The science and practices presented throughout the rest of this chapter are designed to help us all think more deliberately about our connections, engage more intentionally with other people, and embrace a necessary level of vulnerability to meaningfully give of ourselves to others.

# EMBRACE HIGH-QUALITY CONNECTIONS

High-quality connections (HQCs) are defined as short-term, dyadic, positive interactions, defined by a sense of joint participation and responsiveness, positive regard, and even physiologic changes—*hello, social engagement system*—that make us feel more alive.[13] These connections are thought of as a "dynamic, living tissue that exists between two people when there is some contact between them involving mutual awareness."[14] How well this tissue is functioning is marked by the emotional experience of each person within the connection and by the structural features of the connection itself.

Jane Dutton and Emily Heaphy studied and described HQCs in the workplace, but the features of HQCs are certainly applicable in any interaction we have with another person. Unlike low-quality connections, which can be depleting and corrosive, "like black holes, that absorb all the light in the system and give nothing back in return,"[15] HQCs are invigorating, and help both parties within the connection feel seen and cared about.

Imagine how different your day might feel if, instead of feeling tension and awkwardness with your neighbor, coworker, or classmate, your interactions were defined by buoyancy, spontaneity, and open possibilities for action and creativity.[16] All of us can enable more HQCs in our lives by embracing what humanistic psychologist Carl Rogers referred to as "unconditional positive regard,"[17] allowing a person to be who they are with complete acceptance, not trying to limit their own felt experience, but supporting them as they work on their growth.

Reflect: Who in my life might I offer more unconditional positive regard? How might a relationship change if I reoriented my thinking to accept a person for who they are, not who I *want* them to be?

Dutton and her colleagues discuss four primary pathways to actively building HQCs:[18]

1. **Respectful engagement.** Engaging with others in a way that sends a message of value and worth.

- *Be present*. Bring our full attention to the other person. Put that phone away, our email can wait.
- *Listen*. Really listen, not just for the sake of coming up with a response, but to understand what the other person is going through and where they are coming from.
- *Be punctual*. Show up when we say we will. Time is one of the most valuable resources we have—we shouldn't waste another person's.
- *Communicate*. We cannot expect others to read our minds or know how we feel unless we share our feelings explicitly.

2. **Task enabling.** Helping to facilitate another's successful performance through deliberate delegation and empowerment of tasks.
   - *Coach*. Provide training and guidance with clear expectations and feedback.
   - *Facilitate*. Help foster connections for others; match them with opportunities that will optimize their success.
   - *Accommodate*. Be flexible and willing to adjust our expectations to others' needs and circumstances.
   - *Nurture*. When we are warm and approachable, we keep the door open for others to be vulnerable and share what they need with us.

3. **Trusting.** Conveying to another person that they will meet expectations and are dependable.
   - *Self-disclose*. By sharing ourselves with others and modeling vulnerability, we convey, "I trust you with this personal information."
   - *Ask for feedback and proceed accordingly*. When we ask others, "How is this relationship going? What is going well? What can I do differently to help us function better?" and then make changes accordingly, we send the message: "I trust and value your feedback."

4. **Playing.** Participating in activities with the intention of having fun or being playful.
   - *Make time together playful*. Play games with clear rules; do an activity together.

- *Let your guard down.* Share a funny or embarrassing story to reveal your own humanness.
- *Create fun rituals.* Do things for the sake of having fun, even just going for a walk, grabbing a coffee, or seeing a movie together.

HQCs that enable self-disclosure, intimacy, and openness have been shown to increase life satisfaction globally.[19]

## PRACTICE

Spend some time reflecting on a particular connection in your life that is less than high-quality right now.

- Reading through the four pathways to HQCs, which ones might be missing?
- What two or three behaviors or social gestures are within my control that might help improve the quality of the relationship? (Get specific—what can I do and when might I do it?)

Put these behaviors into practice! Be genuine, and experiment with what happens.

- What worked well? How do I know?
- What didn't work so well? How do I know?
- What was the hardest part?
- How can I do better next time?

# SMALL TALK, BIG TALK

After being in and out of quarantines and physically distanced for months on end, many of us have likely felt a bit rusty in social situations (and for some of us, "rusty" is a massive understatement, especially those of us who were not particularly socially inclined to begin with). Even world-renowned psychotherapist Esther Perel admits to feeling this way and writes in her blog about this "social atrophy" that she has experienced on the heels of lockdown.[20] Perel describes reckoning with the sometimes tedious and often superficial work of engaging in small talk, with a newfound appreciation for the craft, reveling in opportunities to engage with local shop clerks, servers, cabdrivers, and fellow restaurant patrons.

By way of easing back into the social worlds we live in, Perel provides some prompts for dipping our toes back into the waters of small talk.

## PRACTICE

### 1. Start with small talk.

- The next time you're in a restaurant, Perel says, consider asking your server: "When you're not working, what's your favorite restaurant around here?"
- Stop into a local shop and ask, "How's business been?"
- Ask your cabdriver, "Where's the most surprising place you've driven to?"
- Ask folks dining at a table next to you, "What did you order? It looks delicious."
- Ask someone on the street, "I love your outfit, where did you get it?"

Asking questions of strangers, when done authentically, shows genuine interest and demonstrates unconditional positive regard. It's also a way to work out our social "muscles." Depending on the situation, we just might make someone's day. See where these conversations lead, how you feel, and how others feel, when you begin to engage this way.

## 2. From small talk to big talk.

On September 10, 2019, organizational psychologist Adam Grant tweeted a #Tuesday thoughts:

> *"Instead of just making small talk, we need more conversations to start with 'big talk.'*

> *"Ask people about their proudest accomplishment, a goal they're pursuing, or an idea that has most intrigued them lately. You'll be surprised by how quickly you can go deep #Tuesdaythoughts."*

Jordyn and her colleague, Dr. Greg Wallingford, a former student of Grant's, turned this idea into an exercise to foster connection in a virtual classroom of medical and graduate students. The simple intervention involves first having students engage with another person in small talk. We provide prompts such as: "Where are you from?" "What did you study in school?" "How did you spend your time during the height of the pandemic?" We then transitioned to big-talk questions, with prompts such as: "What have you most enjoyed working on this year?" "What are you most passionate about outside of work or school?" "What have you learned about yourself or the world during the pandemic?"

While we have no formal scientific evidence to back up this tweet-inspired intervention, when we debriefed the activity, the students reported significantly higher engagement and connection in the big-talk practice compared to small talk and reported learning more about their partners and having more spontaneous, dynamic conversation, rather than simple back-and-forth questions and answers.

Fostering big talk to encourage connection and intimacy is nothing new. In 1997, intimacy researcher Arthur Aron and his team brought strangers into a lab in pairs, matched on their attachment styles, under two different conditions: a small-talk condition, in which subjects engaged in small-talk questions, and a closeness condition (including questions that we consider to be "big talk").[21]

Under both conditions, pairs met and spoke for forty-five minutes. Aron and colleagues found that those in the closeness, or "big talk," group had significantly greater post-interaction closeness compared to those in the small-talk group. Indeed, vulnerability that was "sustained, escalating, reciprocal, personal" through progressively more intimate questions led to greater closeness.

More than twenty years after this experiment, the entire set of big-talk questions used in the study were published in *The New York Times*, titled the "36 Questions that Lead to Love."[22] We recommend that you try these big-talk questions with friends, family members, partners, or even a new prospective partner (first date fodder?), to delve beyond small talk and see what happens when you open yourself up in this way. The small-talk questions are fun too, and may provide a good warm-up, but they will likely not be as effective at building closeness.

Here are a few of our favorite questions you might try out:

| SMALL TALK | BIG TALK |
|---|---|
| 1. What is the best gift you ever received and why? | 1. Given the choice of anyone in the world, whom would you want as a dinner guest? |
| 2. If you had to move from [wherever you live now], where would you go, and what would you miss the most about [where you live now]? | 2. What would constitute a "perfect" day for you? |
| 3. What is the best restaurant you've been to in the last month that your partner hasn't been to? Tell your partner about it. | 3. If you could change anything about the way you were raised, what would it be? |
| 4. What is the best TV show you've seen in the last month that your partner hasn't seen? Tell your partner about it. | 4. If you could wake up tomorrow having gained any one quality or ability, what would it be? |
| 5. What foreign country would you most like to visit? What attracts you to this place? | 5. When did you last cry in front of another person? By yourself? |
| 6. Were you ever in a school play? What was your role? What was the plot of the play? Did anything funny ever happen when you were onstage? | 6. If you were to die this evening with no opportunity to communicate with anyone, what would you most regret not having told someone? Why haven't you told them yet? |

Come up with your own favorite big-talk questions and consider making these questions a part of your conversation repertoire. See what you notice and learn when you commit to moving beyond small talk.

# BE THERE FOR THE GOOD STUFF

One distinct and powerful benefit of close relationships is having others there for us when things are going *right* in our lives.[23] Research shows that the act of communicating positive events that happen to us with others is associated with increased positive affect and well-being, above and beyond the impact of the positive event itself.[24] Additionally, when our good news is met with a particular response style, known as an active-constructive response (ACR), the benefits are enhanced even further (they are *capitalized*)! Studies also reveal that in relationships in which we frequently employ the active-constructive style, partners have greater intimacy and higher relationship satisfaction than partners who use other styles.

So what is the active-constructive response style and how do we use it when others share good news with us? Let's explore four distinct ways of responding, and we'll then delve into ACR.

*The following is based on a true story. Here's the scene: Scott and Jordyn get on a Skype call (yes, Skype, per Scott's insistence, since he is an electronic dinosaur) to start outlining their book. Scott starts the call by sharing some recent good news . . .*

**Scott:** Jordyn, guess what, guess what! I just saw a new apartment right on the beach in Santa Monica. I think I'm going to go for it and try to move in as soon as possible. It really feels like paradise; it's just a few steps from the beach and it even has a great area where I can record my podcast. It's just ideal for this new COVID world we're living in . . . I'm really thrilled about it!

*Now, how might Jordyn have responded?*

A.  I'm glad to hear that, Scott . . . but maybe we can talk about it more later; for now, do you think we can get back to business?
B.  That's great, Scott. Sounds like the setup my old buddy has, he also lives on the beach, but he has this incredible soundproof studio in his basement next to his wine cellar, his own pool, and he's neighbors with the Beckhams . . .
C.  What floor is the place on? If it's the first floor you really have to make sure you have a state-of-the-art security system, and what about all that noise from the beach? Can you even afford this place? Are you sure you want to stay all the way out West for at least another year? Your whole family is on the East Coast . . .
D.  Scott, I am so happy to hear that you've found a place you love! Tell me about it! How did you find it? What's your favorite part? Do you have any pictures to share? I'd love to see it!

| Active-Destructive<br>Quashing the event | Active-Constructive<br>Enthusiastic support, asking questions |
|---|---|
| THE KILLJOY | THE CAPITALIZER |
| Focus on the negative, leads to embarrassment, guilt | Show authentic interest, validation, understanding<br><br>*Strengthens relationships |
| Passive-Destructive<br>Ignoring the event, shift focus to self | Passive-Constructive<br>Quiet, understated support |
| THE ONE-UPPER | THE BUZZKILL |
| Co-opt the conversation, change the topic, turn the focus away from the sharer | *The most destructive to relationships |

Pause and reflect: Using the table above, which responses do you think correspond to which response styles? Do any of the responses make you cringe? Do any sound like responses you've received when you've shared positive news with someone?

Of course, being well versed in the art of ACR, Jordyn's response most closely resembled letter D, the **active-constructive response**. This response style, shown to be the most beneficial to relationship quality, is defined by reacting enthusiastically, asking questions, and showing genuine concern and interest in the positive news. This is the style associated with capitalization, a sort of magnification of the positive experience akin to savoring (see chapter 8). Some people report that with the ACR style, their partners are even more enthused than they are about the event![25]

But what about the other styles? When and why might we fall into these other ways of responding?

A = the **passive-constructive response**. Passive-constructing responding refers to providing quiet, understated support. Partners may be happy for the other person but don't make a big deal out of the positive events, leaving the sharer to think, "My partner is usually silently supportive of me. They might not say much, but I know they are happy for me." We might fall into this response style when we are busy, distracted, or for whatever reason may just not be super-amped for our partner. We might say "Cool!" or "That's great," without further emotional engagement. Although we may think that we are being supportive, this lukewarm response style has been shown to be the most detrimental to relationship quality.

B = the **passive-destructive response**. In this style, the responder may change the topic, seem uninterested in the positive news that is shared, or completely shift the focus of the conversation to something else or even themselves. Essentially, they co-opt and hijack the conversation. In this example, Jordyn "one-upped" Scott by sharing that her friend had an even sweeter setup! We often manifest this style in a well-intentioned attempt to join in with the other person and make a connection, for example, "Oh, I know how you feel because I experienced something similar . . ." However, despite good intentions, the message that's often delivered is more in the realm of, "I don't really care what you have to say right now."

C = the **active-destructive response**. (Shout-out to all the parents or caregivers reading this right now who may recognize, "This sounds like a script between my kids and me!") This response involves shutting down the positive news by pointing out potential holes or problems in a well-intentioned, yet often misguided, effort to protect the sharer. We usually think we are being helpful when we respond this way, but really what we're doing is pointing out the potential downsides of an otherwise good event. In essence, we are quashing our partner's joy.

Of course, not all good news is created equal, and there may be times when pointing out the negatives or bringing a person we care about back down to earth from an unsafe or unrealistic idea might be warranted. However, a steady stream of tempered enthusiasm or seemingly "constructive" criticism can take a toll on the relationship if our partner does not feel supported or if this is all that they hear from us. We can likely all afford to be more deliberate in the ways we respond to others, as small changes toward the ACR style can build a great deal of trust and connection.

## PRACTICE

### 1. Practice ACR.

- Choose someone in your life with whom you are close. Start paying attention to how you respond to them when they relay good news to you. Notice any patterns, especially when you find yourself tending toward the styles other than ACR style.
- Resolve to respond to this person's good news in an active and constructive manner. Find at least three opportunities to use active-constructive responding with this person.
- Reflect on what it feels like, in yourself, and in relation to the other person, to use the ACR style.
  - In what ways was it challenging to modify your response style in this way?
  - How did your partner respond?
  - Did you notice anything change in your relationship dynamic?
  - How can you resolve to use more ACR with this person, and with others, in the future?

## 2. Notice ACR in others.

- Many of us have those people who naturally excel at helping us capitalize on the positive events in our lives. When you are feeling particularly supported by a fellow active-constructive responder, let this person know just how impactful their response is for you. Consider expressing gratitude for their support and for the role that they play in your life.

# GROW TOGETHER

At one time or another, we have all felt insecure in a relationship, whether due to external stressors, unclear communication, or because of our dispositional tendencies toward avoidance or anxiety. However, when partners openly express their fears and needs with one another, and are received with openness, acceptance, and respect, previously silenced concerns can be addressed directly, and partners may be relieved of the pressure to mind-read or to guess how the other person may be feeling.

This practice is designed for dyads (any two individuals: partners, friends, siblings, etc.) to engage in as a framework for deepening valued relationships, demystifying hidden feelings, and securing a foundation of trust and acceptance.

## PRACTICE

### 1. Highlight your relationship superpowers.

- Sit with a partner (a significant other, close friend, etc.) in a comfortable setting without distractions. We recommend putting cellphones away and bringing your full presence to the moment. Together, start by coming up with at least two to three elements of your relationship that you cherish the most, and which bring you the most satisfaction, *e.g.,* the fun you have together, your shared values, an ability to work well together. Feel free to really delve into these elements that make your relationship successful, citing specific memories or stories, perhaps sharing feelings you have not expressed before. In turn, allow each partner a chance to share their reflection.

## 2. Highlight your relationship insecurities.

- Once you both feel that you have a sufficient inventory of the strongest parts of the relationship, allow each partner to share a concern or insecurity that they may be harboring. As you share, agree to the ground rules of using only "I" statements, rather than "you" statements, sharing your experience without placing blame on the other person. For example, instead of saying, "*You are* so rude and inconsiderate for not warning me that you'd be home late," you might share, "*I feel* self-conscious and worried when I don't hear from you about leaving work late; I couldn't sleep."

## 3. Relay mutual understanding.

- The listener will wait to respond in any way until the speaker is entirely done sharing. (This is tricky but effective!) Before responding, the listening partner—without defensiveness or reassurance—then simply repeats back their partner's statement to ensure mutual understanding, for instance, "What I'm hearing is, you are feeling hurt and worried when I don't communicate about when you should expect me home."

## 4. Express thanks.

- Thank one another for expressing these feelings—while it may be difficult to hear something that your partner is insecure about, it takes a ton of bravery to be vulnerable in this way.

## 5. Devise an action plan.

- Together, consider devising a takeaway plan or strategy to address these concerns, drawing upon your mutual strengths from the first part of the exercise to formulate an actionable solution. Even if there is not necessarily something to do about the concerns, a follow-up conversation is a perfectly acceptable plan.

*Note: You will likely not be able to "solve" these problems or concerns in one sitting. The goal of this exercise is to create an environment where it is safe to share feelings directly, practice listening to one another nonjudgmentally and nondefensively, and enable both partners to be more mindful of one another's needs. Drawing upon your strengths together and as a pair can be a great approach to dealing with insecurity and anxiety.*

# FORGIVE

If the COVID era has reminded us of anything, it is perhaps the precariousness of life itself—the limited, precious time we all have on this planet. The idea that we truly never know how much time we have can be simultaneously frightening and liberating: terrifying because we might reckon with how little control we have over our ultimate fate, and empowering by steering us toward the opportunities we do have to live our lives with intention.

Practicing forgiveness of our fellow human beings, and for ourselves, and embracing a broader disposition of *forgivingness*,[26] is one potent mechanism by which we can shed unnecessary toxicity and spend our time on this Earth in greater peace and equanimity. Experiencing hurt from other people is an inevitable part of the human experience. All of us will experience small slights or wrongs at the hands of others, and too many of us will experience deep interpersonal betrayals or trauma (*e.g.*, physical or psychological harm).

One common response to interpersonal trauma is the development of self-deprecating emotions of shame, guilt, worthlessness, powerlessness, and self-blame. These emotions might help mitigate pain in the moment, but they may also have serious emotional costs. Self-blame and shame may fuel a cycle of retraumatization (premature reconciliation, poor boundary-setting), and psychological distress (depression, low self-esteem), especially when self-blame is seen as personal or characterological (*i.e.*, "This happened because I am inherently flawed and worthless") rather than behavioral (*i.e.*, "If I hadn't put myself in this tricky situation, I could have avoided this . . . I will never do that again").[27]

Another common response to interpersonal harm is the development of *self-protective emotions*, such as anger, outrage, indignation, or vengefulness. These emotions may appropriately motivate us to set rigid boundaries and prevent re-trauma, and they may also fuel resentment, bitterness, and revenge-seeking. This response can reinforce a cold, embittered emotional state.

Becoming aware of our own emotional responses to interpersonal offense—*e.g.*, self-deprecating vs. self-protective—is critical for when we commit ourselves to the genuine process of forgiveness.

Pause and reflect:

- How do I typically react when others do wrong by me?
- Do I tend toward self-deprecation, self-protection, or a mixed response? How might my response depend on the situation?
- How do these different responses serve me? How might they stifle my ability to move forward?

Forgiveness is a deliberate, socially motivated process of reducing negative emotions and increasing positive emotions toward a person who has wronged us. Simply reducing negative emotions is necessary but not sufficient for forgiveness. This process also requires acknowledging that a significant transgression has occurred and placing an appropriate level of responsibility on the offender.[28] Only then can we make room to cultivate compassion, benevolence, pity, even love toward the transgressor, and even replace bitter feelings with goodwill. This process reflects the ultimate grace we can give another human being, as receiving forgiveness is not a right, it is a privilege.[29]

A common misconception about forgiveness is that it is an interpersonal process rather than an *intrapersonal* one, but it need not be! We can forgive and still refrain from contacting a transgressor, and we can forgive those who are no longer living. Forgiveness lies within us and only us. Importantly, we can also forgive ourselves for our own misgivings. Forgiveness is not about condoning hurtful behavior; rather, it is about releasing and easing the emotional baggage associated with our pain, so that we do not become crippled by self-destructive thoughts, behaviors, anger, or resentment.

The more adept we become at forgiving, the more we develop *forgivingness*, a general disposition toward forgiveness. Forgivingness is associated with the development of healthy boundaries, effective reconciliation, and resolution of past events, enhanced resilience,[30] and improvements in clinical anxiety and depression.[31]

This practice is adapted from Everett Worthington's REACH model of forgiveness.[32] The five-step model has been widely disseminated and tested and is associated with enhanced emotional forgiveness in diverse populations.[33] REACH is an acronym through which we may free ourselves from the fetters of bitter resentment or self-blame. Before we begin, we must open and commit ourselves to forgive.

## PRACTICE

### R = Recall the hurt.

To forgive, we must first acknowledge that we have experienced hurt at the hands of another person. It is wise to avoid thinking in absolute terms about ourselves as victims and the transgressor as a monster (or ourself as a monster, if we are aiming to forgive ourself). Remember, this is about forgiveness, not retribution. Acknowledge the hurt in a granular way:

- What happened?
- How did this make me feel in the moment?

- What emotions arose for me in the days and weeks after the hurt?
- How am I thinking about the event now?

## E = Empathize with the other person.

Empathy is about putting ourselves in another person's shoes—both emotionally (how they may feel) and cognitively (how they may think). Of course, we can never know exactly what is going on in another's mind unless we ask them, but we can make a genuine effort to try to understand why they may have acted in the way they did.

- Imagine the other person sitting in a chair across from us, ready to listen to what we have to say. Pour our heart out to them. Say—or write—what we would say to that person if they were truly in front of us.

Once we have communicated our feelings, switch positions and imagine that we are the other person. Talk back to yourself in a way that helps make sense of what this person might have been going through when they wronged us. Imagine what might have been going on in that person's life, what they've been through, that enabled them to hurt us.

## A = Altruistic gift.

Determine to give our forgiveness as an unselfish, altruistic gift. To do this, imagine a time when someone in our life forgave us for wrongdoing. How did it feel when we were forgiven?

By forgiving unselfishly, we can allow the person who hurt us to feel that same lightness and freedom.

## C = Commit to forgiveness.

Write a note to yourself to affirm this forgiveness. We may opt for something simple, such as: "Today I forgave [Person's Name] for hurting me." We might consider sharing it with this person, but we can certainly keep this to ourself. Remember, forgiveness is an *intrapersonal* process. Allow this note to serve as our accountability.

**H = Hold on to forgiveness.**

If/when we are feeling in doubt about our forgiveness, reread our note and recommit. Remember, forgiving does not mean forgetting, it simply means letting go of additional pain and hurt after damage has already been done.

After going through these five steps, reflect on this process:

- What did it feel like to engage in this practice?
- Was there a particular step or steps that were the most challenging?
- If you shared your commitment with a person who hurt you, how did it go?
  - How do I feel toward this person now?
- How can I embrace this model to open myself to a disposition of forgivingness?

Feel free to repeat this REACH process with any others in your life who you would like to forgive. Forgiveness is truly one of the most important yet underrated predictors of well-being.[34] On the flip side, an inability to forgive is a very strong marker of narcissism, antagonism, and excessive self-focus.[35] While a healthy self-esteem is a powerful contributor to self-actualization, a narcissistic self-esteem can be a powerful *inhibitor* of self-actualization. Let's now turn our attention to this important topic.

## CHAPTER 3

# Develop Healthy Self-Esteem

All people in our society (with a few pathological exceptions)
have a need or desire for a stable, firmly based,
(usually) high evaluation of themselves, for self-respect,
or self-esteem, and for the esteem of others.
—Abraham Maslow, *A Theory of Human Motivation*

Among everything else that has been "unprecedented" about this era has been the sheer amount of time we've had with our own thoughts. For many of us, the unstable nature of this time has caused extreme self-uncertainty as we manage changes in our environments, including isolation, job losses, and transitioning back and forth between remote work and learning and our physical offices and schools. Of course, the ubiquity of social media provides an unrelenting window into the glamorous lives of other people, celebrities, and our peers, which sends strong and sometimes insidious signals to us about our own lives, taking our focus away from connecting with the people who we truly care about and developing skills that give us a sense of authentic mastery.

In this chapter, we unpack the complex interactions between self-esteem and the need for validation from others. We will help you develop a *healthy self-esteem* as well as a related concept, *self-compassion*, to break down perfectionistic and biased thinking, combat impostor syndrome, and advocate for our own needs.

# WHAT IS A HEALTHY SELF-ESTEEM?

Self-esteem is about liking ourselves, believing that we are worthy, and believing in our own competence—our ability to bring about our own goals through our own actions. This boils down to two core components: self-worth and mastery. Our self-esteem develops early in life in the context of warm caregivers. When children grow up in environments in which they feel that they matter, they internalize the message that they are worthy.[1] Our sense of worthiness is further influenced and molded by the praise and acceptance that we receive from others; our deeply ingrained social protection systems enable us to *feel* the powerful evaluations from others.

However, a *healthy* self-esteem is one in which we develop a relatively stable belief in our self-worth and self-competence that is not so dependent on the momentary evaluations of others. A healthy self-esteem is not about feeling *superior* to others—this would move us more into the territory of narcissism, which we discuss below. Rather, it is about feeling satisfied with and authentically proud of ourselves and our own positive qualities and pursuits. Morris Rosenberg, creator of the Rosenberg Self-Esteem Scale, has said, "When we deal with self-esteem, we are asking whether the individual considers himself adequate—a person of worth—not whether he considers himself superior to others."[2]

We can get a sense of where we stand on these two components of self-esteem by seeing how much we agree with the following statements:[3]

| SELF-WORTH | MASTERY |
|---|---|
| ❏ I like myself. | ❏ I am highly effective at the things I do. |
| ❏ I am a worthwhile human being. | ❏ I am almost always able to accomplish what I try for. |
| ❏ I am very comfortable with myself. | ❏ I perform very well at many things. |
| ❏ I am secure in my sense of self-worth. | ❏ I often fulfill my goals. |
| ❏ I have enough respect for myself. | ❏ I deal well with challenges in my life. |

# HEALTHY SELF-ESTEEM VS. NARCISSISM

While self-esteem is a universal human need, there are various ways humans can regulate this need. Those with a healthy self-esteem believe they are worthy and capable of moving toward their goals in life but aren't so preoccupied with always feeling good about themselves or looking good in their pursuits no matter the cost. Narcissism can be viewed as an *unhealthy regulation of the need for self-esteem*, one whose primary concern is defending an inflated sense of self.

When most people think of narcissism, however, they conjure up a mental image of the supremely confident, chest-thumping narcissist who demands to always be in the spotlight and who is constantly telling us how great and superior they are while simultaneously manipulating and exploiting others. While this is one face of narcissism—referred to as "grandiose narcissism"—psychologists have also identified a more "vulnerable" face of narcissism, characterized by extreme self-uncertainty.

Interestingly, when people take self-esteem surveys, very few people report having *zero* social value. Instead, people low on self-esteem tend to score around the midpoint, suggesting they really have an *uncertain* self-esteem.[4] When extreme self-uncertainty becomes linked to the self-entitlement core of narcissism, high levels of vulnerable narcissism can develop, which often manifests itself by an extreme sensitivity to slights and a deep sense of shame, hostility, distrust, cynicism, and resentment toward others while also requiring constant validation from others; fearing appearing weak or vulnerable; and having grandiose fantasies of receiving respect from others, which often surprise others when they are expressed.[5]

Both grandiose and vulnerable narcissism can cycle back and forth and can even be present simultaneously. Interestingly, research conducted by Scott and his colleague Emmanuel Jauk found a nonlinear relationship between grandiose narcissism and vulnerable narcissism: While in general people with high levels of grandiose narcissism don't tend to report much vulnerable narcissism, there is a "breakpoint" in which *extremely* high levels of grandiose narcissism tend to be more clearly linked to high levels of vulnerable narcissism, which in turn is linked to higher levels of fear, anxiety, and depression.[6]

Since there are such important implications here for our own self-actualization, we think it's worth having extreme honesty with ourselves so that we can work toward removing unnecessary barriers to our growth. Without getting too bogged down by the labels, read the statements below and assess honestly how much these features may be operating in our own daily lives.[7]

| GRANDIOSE NARCISSISM SCALE | VULNERABLE NARCISSISM SCALE |
|---|---|
| ❏ I like being the most popular person at a party. | ❏ I often feel as if I need compliments from others in order to be sure of myself. |
| ❏ I tend to take charge of most situations. | ❏ When I realize I have failed at something, I feel humiliated. |
| ❏ When people judge me, I just don't care. | ❏ When others get a glimpse of my needs, I feel anxious and ashamed. |
| ❏ I often fantasize about having lots of success and power. | ❏ I often hide my needs for fear that others will see me as needy and dependent. |
| ❏ I aspire to greatness. | ❏ I get angry when criticized. |
| ❏ I'm pretty good at manipulating people. | ❏ It irritates me when people don't notice how good a person I am. |
| ❏ I'm willing to exploit others to further my own goals. | ❏ I like to have friends who rely on me because it makes me feel important. |
| ❏ I deserve to receive special treatment. | ❏ Sometimes I avoid people because I'm concerned that they'll disappoint me. |
| ❏ I don't worry about others' needs. | ❏ Sometimes I avoid people because I'm concerned they won't acknowledge what I do for them. |
| ❏ Others say I brag too much, but everything I say is true. | ❏ I often fantasize about being recognized for my accomplishments. |
| | ❏ When someone does something nice for me, I wonder what they want from me. |

Just by virtue of being human, we all agree with some of these statements to some extent! In fact, some of these are highly adaptive coping strategies for protecting ourselves from the painful experience of rejection from others and from our own self-judgment and shame. To have some narcissistic characteristics is to be human. We each have the potential to dip into the terrain of narcissism, and our narcissistic concerns can fluctuate wildly even throughout the course of a single day.

Regardless of our overall patterns, we can all work on keeping these characteristics in check so that they don't overshadow our highest potentials. There's nothing wrong with having great ambitions or being confident. The problem is being *overly* confident (in the case of grandiose narcissism) or having intense *shame* over being ambitious (in the case of vulnerable narcissism). Overconfidence can lead to errors and ignoring real feedback that can help us grow. Research conducted by Scott and his colleagues clearly shows that vulnerable narcissism is associated with lower levels of life satisfaction, sense of autonomy, authenticity, mastery, personal growth, positive social relationships, purpose, and self-acceptance in life, as well as a lack of trust in one's thoughts and feelings, a profound lack of a sense of self, and, as we'll discuss more later, high levels of impostor syndrome.[8]

We'd like to offer a healthier alternative to the narcissistic attitude toward oneself that is sustainable and more likely to lead to growth and positive connections with others: self-compassion.

## HEALTHY SELF-ESTEEM AND SELF-COMPASSION

> It seems to me that the [fully functioning] individual moves toward being, knowingly and acceptingly, the process which he inwardly and actually is . . . He is not trying to be more than he is, with the attendant feelings of insecurity or bombastic defensiveness. He is not trying to be less than he is, with the attendant feelings of guilt or self-deprecation. He is increasingly listening to the deepest recesses of his physiological and emotional being, and finds himself increasingly willing to be, with greater accuracy and depth, that self which he most truly is.
>
> —Carl Rogers, *On Becoming a Person:*
> *A Therapist's View of Psychotherapy*

If self-esteem is an authentic evaluation of our self-worth and mastery, what happens when we are not feeling particularly masterful, or face the inevitable setbacks of human existence? Many modern psychologists, a leader among them world self-compassion expert Kristin Neff, pose that *self-compassion*, the practice of treating ourselves with kindness, recognizing our shared humanity, and being mindful when considering negative aspects of ourselves, provides an appealing alternative to focusing on always feeling good about ourselves.

Self-compassion is a resource that is there for us even through inevitable hardship and suffering. If self-esteem is based in performance evaluation or "getting it right," Neff says, self-compassion is about "opening our hearts"[9]—treating ourselves like we would treat a dear friend. Even the most highly successful and widely accomplished people on the planet sometimes feel like phonies or impostors—that their success has been a result of luck, rather than from their own mastery and skill. How many of us can be our own harshest critics? How many of us actually treat ourselves the same way we would treat a close friend in need? We often are so *cold* to ourselves. Self-compassion enables us to be with our painful experiences and yet radically accept our whole selves despite them.

In her book *Fierce Self-Compassion* and in many of her scientific publications on the subject, Neff emphasizes the distinction between self-compassion and self-esteem, exposing some of the shortcomings of self-esteem, or, rather, the tactics that many of us may use to bolster our self-esteem, for instance, raising ourselves up by putting others down, judging our own worth by arbitrary standards that we set for ourselves leading to distorted self-perceptions,[10] and displaying prejudice[11] and even violence toward people who threaten our egos.[12]

"[Self-compassion] allows us to be fully human," Neff says.

*We give up trying to be perfect or lead an ideal life, and instead focus on caring for ourselves in every situation. I may have just missed my deadline or said something foolish or made a poor decision, and my self-esteem may have taken a big hit, but if I'm kind and understanding toward myself in those moments, I've succeeded. When we can accept ourselves as we are, giving ourselves support and love, then we've achieved our goal. It's a box that can always be checked, no matter what.[13]*

## THE YIN AND YANG OF SELF-COMPASSION

Neff draws upon the ancient Chinese philosophical concept of the yin and yang—the universal energetic principle reflecting the fine balance of stillness and movement—to describe two distinct energies that comprise self-compassion.

As yin represents a soft, yielding, receptive, nurturing energy, the yin quality of self-compassion is tender; it involves being present with and accepting ourselves, soothing, validating, and reassuring ourselves that we are not alone in our suffering. Neff describes yin as the "healing power" of self-compassion. The complementary force, the yang, is fierce, protective, and motivating. Neff describes the yang as a "momma bear turned inward," acting in the world to alleviate suffering. When we practice self-compassion, we can utilize practical wisdom as to when it is time to practice acceptance, embracing the yin, and when we must call upon the yang to protect ourselves and act in the world.

**Yin and Yang self-compassion:**
Using caring force to change ourselves and our world

Being with ourselves

**Yang:**
- Protecting
- Providing
- Motivating

Acting in the world

**Yin:**
- Comforting
- Soothing
- Validating

Pause and reflect:

- How do these concepts resonate with me? In what situations has my self-esteem been threatened, and how might it have been helpful to practice self-compassion?
- What situations in my life require me to practice the yin (tender, soothing, validating) element of self-compassion?
- What situations in my life require me to practice the yang (fierce, protecting, motivating) element of self-compassion?

The remainder of this chapter presents practices aimed at bolstering our healthy self-esteem through the lens of self-compassion, without the need for a narcissistic self-presentation. How do we set appropriate boundaries with others, combat a pervasive feeling of impostorism, and understand our own self-defeating thought patterns to engage more optimally in the world around us? While these practices are first and foremost for us as individuals, they are intended to help us on our path toward making our communities and the world a better place. Changing the world starts from within. Let's grow.

## SET HEALTHY BOUNDARIES

When you say "yes" to something,
you are always saying "no" to something else.[14]
—Gail Gazelle, M.D., physician coach

In times of change and uncertainty, it is critical that we practice advocating for our own needs, setting firm personal boundaries and learning to say "no" when we need to. Protecting and advocating for ourselves is an example of what Neff calls *fierce self-compassion*.[15] This fierceness (the yang) must be accompanied by a warm, loving, and connected presence with ourselves (the yin), as it is "being with" ourselves that enables us to authentically connect with our needs in the first place.[16]

In fact, prioritizing our own needs and goals, and asserting these needs more regularly, is an excellent strategy we can use to give to others more effectively.[17] Scott developed a "healthy selfishness scale" that breaks down the false dichotomy that we are *either* selfish when helping ourselves or unselfish when helping others. Scott found that healthy selfishness is correlated with several indicators of growth, including a healthy self-esteem, life satisfaction, and authentic pride in one's work. Paradoxically, those scoring higher in healthy selfishness were more likely to care about others and reported more growth-oriented motivations for helping others, such as, "A main reason why I help others is a desire for personal growth," and, "I like helping others because it genuinely makes me feel good to help others grow." Consider the items below and see how much healthy selfishness you have in your own life (you might decide you could use quite a bit more healthy selfishness!):

HEALTHY SELFISHNESS SCALE[18]
- ❏ I have healthy boundaries.
- ❏ I have a lot of self-care.
- ❏ I have a healthy dose of self-respect and don't let people take advantage of me.
- ❏ I balance my own needs with the needs of others.
- ❏ I advocate for my own needs.
- ❏ I have a healthy form of selfishness (*e.g.*, meditation, eating healthy, exercising) that does not hurt others.
- ❏ Even though I give a lot to others, I know when to recharge.
- ❏ I give myself permission to enjoy myself, even if it doesn't necessarily help others.
- ❏ I take good care of myself.
- ❏ I prioritize my own personal projects over the demands of others.

We're sure you've heard the trope on any flight you've ever taken: "Put your oxygen mask on yourself before helping others." This is a wise truism that we can all embrace in many facets of our lives. How can we possibly give to others sustainably if we are not first tending to our own needs?

So how do we go about prioritizing our own needs and goals, saying "no" more effectively, and setting healthy boundaries with others? Doing this well requires *healthy assertiveness*, a social skill defined by open, honest, and respectful communication, in which we express our needs, wants, and feelings directly, while welcoming and even embracing the needs of others, including those with opposing viewpoints.

We can all practice adopting a more assertive communication style by understanding the mindset of healthy assertiveness. Individuals who have mastered this style tend to operate under the assumption that others' needs are just as important as—but not necessarily more important than—their own, and that everyone has something valuable to contribute. The goal of healthy assertiveness is to maintain self-respect and respect for others, while forgoing the need to "win" all the time.

Practicing healthy assertiveness involves recognizing our own worth and accepting that we can control only our own behavior, not the behavior of others. People are not mind readers; if we want something, we have to ask for it! Doing so in a clear and straightforward manner reduces ambiguity and makes our wants clear: *"I'd love it if you can please call me when your meeting ends so I know what time to expect you home,"* or, *"Can you please let me know exactly when you need this by so that I can prepare accordingly?"*

> **People are not mind readers; if we want something, we have to ask for it!**

When we don't want something or need to say "no," we must also do so directly. *"I'm so grateful you thought of me for this project; unfortunately, now is not a good time for me."* You may even consider adding a statement such as, *"I'm afraid I can't go out tonight; I am giving myself some much-needed self-care time."* When we say "no" in service of self-care, Neff advocates, we model the important message that we are each responsible for our own well-being, and we give others permission to do the same.

For those of us who may not know how we feel in the moment when someone is asking something of us, instead of defaulting to the knee-jerk *"of course I'll do it!"* we might employ the "let me think about it" strategy,[19] that is, *"Let me think it over and I'll get back to you by the end of the week."* Sometimes, and especially for those of us who tend to be "yes" people, we need that bit of space to weigh the value of a task. Setting a clear expectation of when we will get back to the person can put a healthy amount of pressure on ourselves to make our decision in a timely manner.

An assertive style is one of four primary communication styles, which include passive, aggressive, passive-aggressive, and assertive. Characteristics of these primary styles, including behaviors, nonverbals, beliefs, emotions, and goals, are summarized in the figure below, adapted from Randy Paterson's *The Assertiveness Workbook*.[20] This practice is about beginning to actualize our fierce self-compassion and healthy assertiveness in favor of these other, less adaptive communication styles.

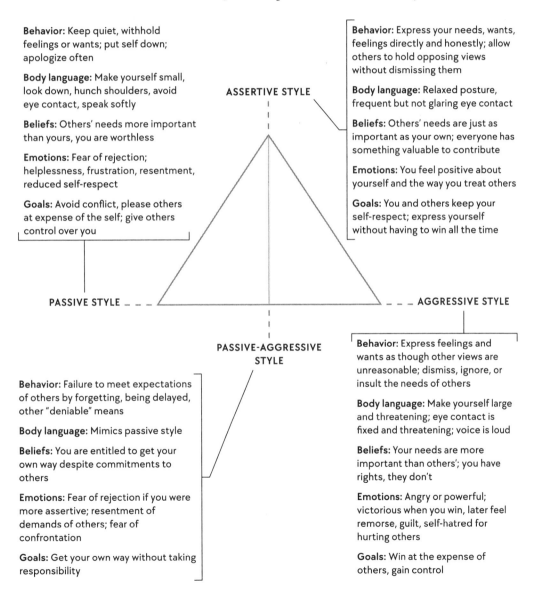

**Behavior:** Keep quiet, withhold feelings or wants; put self down; apologize often

**Body language:** Make yourself small, look down, hunch shoulders, avoid eye contact, speak softly

**Beliefs:** Others' needs more important than yours, you are worthless

**Emotions:** Fear of rejection; helplessness, frustration, resentment, reduced self-respect

**Goals:** Avoid conflict, please others at expense of the self; give others control over you

**ASSERTIVE STYLE**

**Behavior:** Express your needs, wants, feelings directly and honestly; allow others to hold opposing views without dismissing them

**Body language:** Relaxed posture, frequent but not glaring eye contact

**Beliefs:** Others' needs are just as important as your own; everyone has something valuable to contribute

**Emotions:** You feel positive about yourself and the way you treat others

**Goals:** You and others keep your self-respect; express yourself without having to win all the time

**PASSIVE STYLE**

**AGGRESSIVE STYLE**

**PASSIVE-AGGRESSIVE STYLE**

**Behavior:** Failure to meet expectations of others by forgetting, being delayed, other "deniable" means

**Body language:** Mimics passive style

**Beliefs:** You are entitled to get your own way despite commitments to others

**Emotions:** Fear of rejection if you were more assertive; resentment of demands of others; fear of confrontation

**Goals:** Get your own way without taking responsibility

**Behavior:** Express feelings and wants as though other views are unreasonable; dismiss, ignore, or insult the needs of others

**Body language:** Make yourself large and threatening; eye contact is fixed and threatening; voice is loud

**Beliefs:** Your needs are more important than others'; you have rights, they don't

**Emotions:** Angry or powerful; victorious when you win, later feel remorse, guilt, self-hatred for hurting others

**Goals:** Win at the expense of others, gain control

# PRACTICE

1. **Reflect.** Review the pyramid graphic and the behaviors, body language, beliefs, emotions, and goals of the passive, passive-aggressive, aggressive, and assertive styles. Without judging ourselves, consider honestly where we fall along this pyramid in most domains of our lives. (Note, *we may demonstrate different styles in different contexts or with different people; think about your most dominant style.*) Depending on your dominant style, complete the following reflection:

| FOR THE PASSIVE COMMUNICATOR | FOR THE PASSIVE-AGGRESSIVE COMMUNICATOR | FOR THE AGGRESSIVE COMMUNICATOR | FOR THE ASSERTIVE COMMUNICATOR |
|---|---|---|---|
| 1. In what ways do my own needs and wants matter just as much as other people's? | 1. In what ways might I expect others to "read my mind" based on my actions, instead of telling them how I feel directly? | 1. How might I practice creating more space for the needs and wants of others? | 1. In what ways does my assertive communication serve my sense of well-being and the quality of my relationships with others? |
| 2. How might more clearly advocating for my own needs better serve me and my goals? How might this better serve the groups and teams that I am a part of? | 2. How might more clearly advocating for my own needs better serve me and my goals? How might this better serve the groups and teams that I am a part of? | 2. In what ways might I benefit from better understanding the needs and wants of other people? How might this benefit the groups and teams that I am a part of? | 2. Are there any areas of my life in which it is particularly challenging for me to be assertive? If so, which domains and how so? |
| 3. In what ways might I set firmer boundaries with others so that I feel less resentful, more in control, and more satisfied with myself? | 3. In what ways might I be more direct in expressing my needs and wants? | 3. In what ways might I demonstrate, through behaviors and my body language, that I value others' needs and wants? | 3. In what ways might I practice embracing an assertive style in these other domains? |

For *everyone*: Consider a situation or a relationship in your life in which you would like to be more assertive (and less passive, passive-aggressive, or aggressive). Think across different domains, including home, work, social life, etc. Perhaps you can afford to say "no" in service of your own self-care or set a healthy boundary with someone or something that is taking up too much of your emotional, spiritual, or physical energy.

- Bring this person or situation into your mind's eye and hold it there for a few moments. You may close your eyes as you imagine this situation to bring it into clearer focus.
- While holding this image in your mind, begin to invite a settled presence to your mind and body. Take several deep breaths from your belly and welcome a sense of warmth and calm to wash over you. Just sit with yourself for a few moments, allowing yourself to fully explore and validate your needs in this situation.
- Come up with one or two sentences that capture this need as directly and firmly (though not rudely) as possible. Exclude any apologies, especially if you tend toward a more passive style. Rehearse these sentences in your mind, and, even better, write them down. Ask yourself: *What is my goal, and how can I communicate it as clearly, directly, and concisely as possible?*
- Set yourself up to share this sentiment with the relevant parties, exactly as you practiced. Be sure to include assertive, respectful body language.

2. **Go out and set the boundary!** Listen carefully to the response you receive when you share your need in the manner that you practiced. Vow to respect the opinion that is shared back to you, without arguing or recoiling. Catch yourself if you find that you are defaulting into passive, passive-aggressive, or aggressive responses, body language, or beliefs. If you meet resistance, take a breath and maintain your settled body. Without compromising your own values or needs, perhaps consider revisiting the issue later.

3. **Reflect on this experience:**
   - What did I do? How did it go?
   - What, if anything, was particularly challenging? What went well?

- How did it feel to advocate directly for my own needs and wants while maintaining respect for another person's goals or needs?
- What, if anything, might I do differently next time?
- How can I continue to maintain healthy boundaries in this way?

# CHALLENGE DISTORTED THINKING

Since COVID-19 came on the scene, life for many of us has been riddled with pervasive and prolonged uncertainty; genuine threats to our safety, health, and survival; and a reimagining of life as we knew it. This has been the perfect recipe for "cognitive distortions," or biased habitual errors in our thinking, to manifest in full force and magnify the fear and chaos of this time. This practice is about identifying and understanding some of the cognitive distortions that we fall subject to, and actively challenging and testing the validity of them so that we may break negative thought patterns, employ reason, and nurture perspectives that serve our growth, not just our survival.[21] In doing so, we can practice bringing a sense of curiosity to our automatic thoughts and core beliefs, and meet them with rationality and self-kindness.

Common cognitive distortions, with their definitions and examples, are summarized in the table on the following pages. Questions to challenge such distortions are included as well.[22]

## PRACTICE

1. **Develop insight.** Read through the table of common cognitive distortions and pick out those that you find yourself falling subject to regularly.
   - Which distortions do I fall into most commonly?
   - When do I typically fall into these thinking patterns? Are there particular situations, internal states or moods, or people with whom I fall subject to these patterns?

2. **Be a scientist!** Use the table, adapted from Aaron Beck's Daily Record of Dysfunctional Thoughts,[23] to think about specific examples when we got caught in a cognitive distortion recently. Dissect the scenario, from the trigger or activating event we experienced to the automatic thoughts that arose, to the resultant consequences. Consequences may be emotional (how did I feel?), behavioral (what did I do?), and physiological (what happened in my body?). Challenge these distortions using the critical questions we provided. Also consider: *What would I say to a friend who is experiencing something similar?* Finally, explore how you feel after disputing these distortions.

3. **Catch distortions in real time!** Embrace a regular habit of noting and intervening on cognitive distortions as they arise to replace negative emotions, behaviors, and physiologic responses with more favorable, rational, adaptive, and self-compassionate ones.

| DISTORTION | DEFINITION | DATING LIFE EXAMPLE | COVID-RELATED EXAMPLE | CRITICAL QUESTIONS TO CHALLENGE DISTORTIONS |
|---|---|---|---|---|
| **All-or-Nothing Thinking** | Viewing everything in extreme terms | "If I get rejected by this woman, I'm a total loser in life." | "If I mess up this job interview, I will never be able to find work again; my family will starve, and we will have no hope of getting out of this." | What might the gray area be here? |

| DISTORTION | DEFINITION | DATING LIFE EXAMPLE | COVID-RELATED EXAMPLE | CRITICAL QUESTIONS TO CHALLENGE DISTORTIONS |
|---|---|---|---|---|
| **Catastrophizing** | Believing that the worst will happen in a given situation | *"If I approach this woman I really like, I am 100 percent going to get rejected harshly and everyone will see and I will feel totally humiliated and the video of this happening will appear on Instagram somewhere and my mom will see and . . ."* | *"If I can't send my children to school, they are not going to learn anything all year, and they will become totally emotionally and developmentally stunted, and they will never recover and achieve their potential, and they will be doomed to be failures in life . . ."* | How likely is it that this worst-case scenario will happen? What evidence do I have to believe that this will happen? Do I have a sense of agency here to improve the outcome? |
| **False Sense of Hopelessness** | Believing we have less power to reach an outcome than we really do | *"There's no point in approaching her anyway; I'll probably just come across as shady."* | *"I shouldn't even bother talking to my boss about needing to take some time to find childcare . . . they are just going to fire me anyway; I might as well quit . . ."* | What could come of taking a risk here, even if the odds of success are low? |

| DISTORTION | DEFINITION | DATING LIFE EXAMPLE | COVID-RELATED EXAMPLE | CRITICAL QUESTIONS TO CHALLENGE DISTORTIONS |
|---|---|---|---|---|
| **Minimizing** | Undervaluing our role in positive events | *"She seems interested in me, but I don't think I really deserve it . . . It was probably my new jacket she really liked and not anything I said or did in that interaction."* | *"Our team did well on the virtual presentation—it was all because of the work my colleagues put in; I am really dead weight on this team."* | What could I have done to contribute to the situation? |
| **Personalizing** | Attributing the outcome of a situation as solely the result of one's own actions or behaviors | *"She said she has a boyfriend; she must be saying that because she really is not interested in me and was probably repulsed by me."* | *"If I were only a better parent, my kid wouldn't be having such a hard time with this remote-learning thing. What is wrong with me; why can't I get it together?"* | What could others have done to contribute to the situation? |
| **Should-ing** | Thinking the way we want things to turn out is how they ought to have turned out | *"She really should have liked me; it seemed so meant-to-be."* | *"I really shouldn't feel so down right now, no one in my family is sick."* | Is this thought rational? Why "should" it have happened this way? What evidence do I have that things "should" have turned out differently? |

| DISTORTION | DEFINITION | DATING LIFE EXAMPLE | COVID-RELATED EXAMPLE | CRITICAL QUESTIONS TO CHALLENGE DISTORTIONS |
|---|---|---|---|---|
| **Entitlement** | Expecting a particular outcome based on our status or behavior | "I deserve for her to like me because I'm such a nice guy." | "I get that the rule is that we should wear masks at work, but I just tested negative so I shouldn't have to." | Is this thought rational? What makes me think that I deserved a different outcome? |
| **Jumping to Conclusions** | Feeling certain of the meaning of a situation despite little evidence to support that conclusion | "She hasn't texted me back in two days; I know that she is actively trying to avoid me . . ." | "My boss asked me to meet randomly later today . . . I know I'm going to get fired for being sick last week." | What might be an alternative explanation? What evidence do I have? |
| **Overgeneralizing** | Drawing conclusions or settling on a global belief based on a single situation | "Since I was rejected by her, I might as well never approach any other woman I'm interested in ever again because I am obviously unlovable." | "Anyone who doesn't wear a mask in the grocery store just doesn't care about the well-being of others." | Is this a fair global assessment? |
| **Mind Reading** | Assuming others know what you are thinking or that you know what another is thinking, despite not communicating directly | "She should know that I am interested in her romantically; it doesn't need to be said." | "My friend should just know that I don't feel comfortable eating indoors; I shouldn't have to tell her before she makes our dinner reservation." | Was I clear in communicating? Am I missing critical information? |

| DISTORTION | DEFINITION | DATING LIFE EXAMPLE | COVID-RELATED EXAMPLE | CRITICAL QUESTIONS TO CHALLENGE DISTORTIONS |
|---|---|---|---|---|
| **Emotional Reasoning** | Reasoning that what we feel is true, without evidence | *"I feel jealous when I see my new partner talking to other guys . . . She must be cheating on me, or why else would I feel this way?"* | *"I feel infuriated when I see folks unmasked in indoor places. I just know that they have no respect for anyone else and that they must not know anyone who has died from this virus."* | Do my feelings accurately reflect the facts of the situation? |
| **Outsourcing Happiness** | Giving outside factors the ultimate arbiter of our happiness | *"I can't be happy in life unless I am attractive to women."* | *"I just can't be happy until my kids go back to school."* | How can I rely on my inner self for happiness in this moment? |

**SITUATION:** Briefly describe the activating event leading up to an unpleasant emotion, behavior, or physiologic response.

*Automatic Thought:* What automatic thought(s) came to mind to accompany the emotion?

*Cognitive Distortion(s):* What cognitive distortion(s) are present in each automatic thought?

*Consequence(s):* Specify the emotion(s), behavior(s), and physiologic responses that you experienced in the aftermath of the event.

*Rational, Self-compassionate Response:* What is a more rational, realistic way of viewing the situation? Consider what you might tell a good friend who is in your shoes.

*Outcome(s):* Specify the emotion(s), behavior(s), and physiologic responses you are experiencing after noting and questioning the cognitive distortion. How do you feel now?

# BREAK THE IMPOSTOR CYCLE

Many of us tend to fall victim to one cognitive trap called the impostor phenomenon (IP), which refers to feelings of doubt, fear, apprehension, and shame that lead us to undermine our own abilities and the worthiness of our own success. This phenomenon was first described in the 1970s by psychologists Pauline Rose Clance and Suzanne Imes. When Clance was a graduate student, she often worried that despite adequate preparation, she would fail her examinations. As her friends grew tired of hearing these seemingly ridiculous fears, she felt the need to keep these self-defeating feelings to herself.[24] Later, as a counselor at a liberal arts college, Clance observed that even among the highest-achieving students, particularly women, there was a pervasive undercurrent of feeling like a phony or intellectual fraud, and a fear of being uncovered as an impostor among one's highly talented and accomplished peers.[25] Though first observed in professional women, impostorism has since been seen across various genders and cultural groups.[26] If you have felt this way, you are far from alone; though estimates across studies vary widely by population and method, up to 82 percent of those sampled in studies have experienced impostorism.[27]

Interestingly, Scott and his colleagues found a particularly strong correlation between impostorism and vulnerable narcissism.[28] This does *not* mean that if you experience impostor syndrome you are also likely to score high in narcissism. It does mean, however, that if you identify strongly with the items on the vulnerable narcissism scale, you may be more likely to *report* that you suffer from impostor syndrome. For these individuals, it's not that they necessarily feel fraudulent, but that they are engaging in a self-presentation strategy that serves as a way of protecting themselves against the potential pain of rejection.[29] By telling others they feel like an impostor, they can adjust the expectations of others and won't feel as much shame if they do not succeed. Ultimately, however, this approach may stunt growth. Therefore, the practice in this section can help *anyone*, including those whose impostorism may even be coming from a place of narcissistic vulnerability.

Read through the following statements, adapted from the Clance Impostor Phenomenon Scale, to get a rough sense of your tendencies toward impostorism.[30]

❏ When people praise me for something I've accomplished, I'm afraid I won't be able to live up to their expectations in the future.

❏ I sometimes think I obtained my present position or success because I happened to be in the right place at the right time, because I knew the right people, because of some kind of error, or because of some kind of external circumstance.

❏ I tend to remember the incidents when I have not done my best more than those times I have done my best.

❏ Sometimes I'm afraid that people will discover how much knowledge or ability I really lack.

❏ I often compare my ability to those around me and think they may be more intelligent than I am.

Since Clance first wrote about the topic, the impostor phenomenon has been widely discussed and studied. It is believed to develop in tandem with perfectionism,[31] a strong need to please others,[32] and family environments of low support and emotional expression and high levels of control, anger, and conflict.[33] Such early-life dynamics are reinforced through socialization for achievement in adolescence and adulthood. The phenomenon has been shown to contribute to psychological distress, including anxiety and depression[34] and correlate with an uncertain self-esteem and, as already mentioned, vulnerable narcissism.[35]

A core feature includes what Clance has called the Impostor Cycle, which begins when we are tasked with things related to our achievement (for instance, a job interview, a major assignment at work, writing this book). Such a request can unmask underlying anxiety, fear of failure, and self-doubt (*"Am I even qualified for this?"*), which may lead to one of two paths: overpreparation or procrastination. When the task is ultimately done—perhaps we get the job, make the big presentation, or deliver the manuscript—we feel an immense, albeit temporary, sigh of relief. For those of us who choose the overpreparation route (Jordyn is admittedly guilty of this), we attribute our success to effort (*"I just worked my butt off . . . Anyone can do this if they try!"*). For those of us who choose procrastination mode—and subsequent frenzied preparation when the clock starts ticking (ahem, Scott)—we may attribute our positive results to luck or outside forces.

This habit of discounting our own capabilities and attributing our success to either effort or luck reinforces self-doubt and a core belief that accomplishment by hard work alone does not reflect true ability. These beliefs imbue feelings of fraudulence (*"When are they going to find out I'm a phony?"*) and high levels of anxiety when we are faced with achievement-oriented tasks in the future.[36] The figure below summarizes this Impostor Cycle.[37]

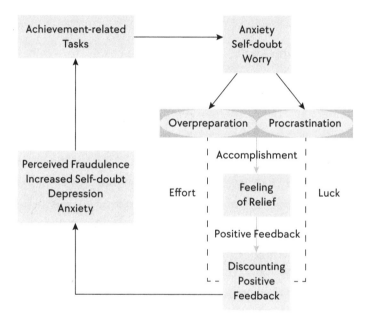

For some of us, the impostor phenomenon is activated when we realize that we may not be as exceptional relative to others as we once thought we were. For instance, as we make our way up the ranks through our education, from middle and high school, potentially to college and even graduate school or the workplace, we may discover just how excellent other people are and, therefore, no longer view ourselves as quite as special. For those of us who tend toward impostorism, instead of the awe or adoration we might feel when we are surrounded by such extraordinary people, we feel insecure in our own abilities. Rather than a display of false modesty, impostorism involves a genuine fear of failure or unworthiness and real difficulty internalizing our own goodness and worth.

What's so interesting is that even the most accomplished experts can feel this way;

in fact, highly accomplished people as well as marginalized groups—who in many cases have had to work even harder for the success they've achieved—may be even more likely to feel like impostors. So what do we do about it? How do we break this draining impostor cycle?

Perhaps healing from our impostorism requires *owning it*: identifying and naming it, embracing our "beginner's mind" by finding strength and opportunity in what we don't know, asking for help, and reflecting on how the results we earn do accurately reflect our own abilities.

Let's break the Impostor Cycle.

## PRACTICE

1. Take a moment to reflect on how impostorism shows up in your life. Consider a recent time when you may have gotten caught in the Impostor Cycle.
   - When did I last feel like an impostor? What were some of the thoughts, emotions, behaviors, and bodily sensations that arose for me when I was stuck in this cycle?
   - Do I tend to fall more into procrastination mode or overpreparation mode? Are there other behaviors I adopt?
   - In what ways do these impostor feelings hinder me from going after my goals?
   - How might various facets of my identity (my gender, race, ethnicity, professional or family roles, etc.) intersect with these impostor feelings?
   - What does it feel like when I achieve the goal? To what extent do I attribute my success to external factors or hard work, rather than my own abilities?

2. Now imagine that a close friend of yours discloses to you that they feel like an impostor. They feel everything that you yourself are feeling.
   - How might I comfort and soothe them? What would I say?
   - How might I help them fiercely advocate for themselves and their abilities?
   - How might I turn some of these sentiments inward toward myself? In other words, how can I practice self-compassion to interrupt the Impostor Cycle in my own life?

3. Now consider how doubting our abilities to some extent might be protective against hubris and misleading overconfidence.
   - How might I embrace my "beginner's mind," or the idea that a lack of experience or expertise may help me view situations more clearly, openly, and flexibly, without preconceived notions or bias?
   - How might I leverage my beginner's mind to my advantage in the future?
   - Is there anyone who I might reach out to in the future to help me be a better learner and fill some of my own knowledge gaps to intercept the Impostor Cycle?

4. Finally, bring into your mind's eye one of the wisest people you know, someone who you consider to be an expert in a topic or domain that you are passionate about. Imagine this person as a child and visualize them growing up into the person and expert they are today. How might this evolution have happened? Do you imagine that they have ever doubted their own abilities? How might effort or circumstances have played into their success?

Consider reaching out to this person and asking them some of these questions. Have they ever felt like an impostor? What advice do they have for you as you emerge on your own journey toward breaking this cycle?

# DITCH PERFECT

This is a book about incremental, sustained growth, *not* perfection or instant "hacks." And yet, on this quest to develop ourselves and grow from adversity, it can be all too compelling to fall into the trap of thinking we have to grow *perfectly*—that this process is an all-or-nothing endeavor, that we will either succeed at it or fail. However, this is far from the case; in fact, *failure* is an essential part of growth, and remember: Life is not a video game. We never reach a "level" and hear some voice from above saying, "Congratulations, you've unlocked the next level of life!" Life is often a two-steps-forward, one-step-back process, of which mistakes and, yes, even failure, are an integral part.[38]

Perhaps you picked up this book in the first place because you believe that you can be a "better person," that you *should* feel better about your life, or that your life will somehow fundamentally change if you would only strive bigger, work harder, or achieve more. Some of these thoughts might reveal an underlying predilection toward perfectionism.

**Failure *is an essential part of growth*.**

Here are some questions that can also tease out this tendency:

- Am I satisfied with doing my best, or am I disappointed by anything short of perfect?
- Do I have incredibly high standards for myself and judge myself or feel down when I do not meet these standards?
- Do I have incredibly high standards for others?
- Do I tend to be more motivated by a fear of failure or by a genuine interest in pursuing my goals?
- Am I more focused on the results of my goals or on the process of working toward my goals?
- Do I tend to hyper-focus on *how* I am doing, at the expense of losing myself in *what* I am doing?

Perfectionism can often come at the expense of vulnerability and deep engagement with the parts of ourselves that are truly works in progress (in the next chapter, we will help you to explore and embrace your "dark" side). Folks who fall into the perfectionism trap tend to overvalue accomplishment, continuously strive to be "better" at the expense of contentment, and set incredibly high, even unrealistic, expectations of themselves and others. This tendency is frequently driven by external pressures (expectations of others, such as our parents, our educational environments, our boss) and then internalized and reinforced by our own hardwired desire to avoid failure, worthlessness, and self-doubt.

These days, social media is another powerful driver, where the norm is to present a persona of perfection (and where everyone looks like an airbrushed Disney princess with perfect bodies and perfect cocktails in their perfect hands!). The ubiquity of apparent perfection on social media certainly distorts our reality, and leaves us mere mortals thinking, *"If everyone has their shit so together, what is wrong with me?"*

The perfectionism trap can leave us feeling exhausted, isolated, and constantly dissatisfied with ourselves and others. No matter the precise origin of the high standards we are subject to, definitions of success and failure are usually accompanied by predictable cycles of reward or punishment. As shown in the perfectionism figure below (that Jordyn developed with her dear friend and collaborator, psychiatrist Dr. Annie Hart),[39] when we don't meet the unrealistic expectations, we might think that we are worthless and experience shame, anxiety, and existential disappointment. This trap can lead us to take constructive criticism defensively, procrastinate and avoid challenges, and, in turn, be even less productive. It may even lead us, ironically, to compensation mode, setting even higher expectations of ourselves in the future.

In those times when we *do* meet unrealistic expectations, this can be incredibly reinforcing; for a fleeting time, this validation may instill fragile pride and further reinforce our fear of failure. We might strive to work even harder and continue chasing perfection, with costs to our self-worth and well-being. This ostensible success sets us on a pathway toward what we call "I'll be happy when . . ." syndrome—the elusive phenomenon of thinking we will be happy when we just meet that next goal, get that promotion, or achieve more success.

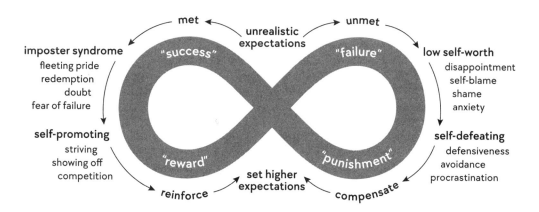

This practice is about questioning the pressures that we place on ourselves and receive from others to be perfect and settle for "I'm a work in progress; mistakes are inevitable," so that we disentangle our notions of failure and success with honest growth and fulfillment.

# PRACTICE

1. Spend some time quietly reflecting on the following prompts. Think broadly and across domains of your life (personally, professionally, socially, etc.).
   - What are some of the expectations that *others* have of me right now (implicitly or explicitly)?
     - How realistic are these expectations? How are others expecting me to be perfect?
   - What are some of the expectations that I have of *myself* right now? In other words, are there things that you tell yourself you *should* be doing on a regular basis?
     - How realistic are these expectations? In what ways might I be—consciously or not—expecting myself to be "perfect"?
   - Who has harsher or higher expectations of me? Others or myself? How do others' expectations of me inform my expectations of me? How does the pressure to be perfect impact my performance? What does it feel like to feel that I have to meet such high standards? What are the emotional costs? What are the behavioral costs? What are the costs to my energy? My sense of self-worth?

2. After reflecting on these questions, review the following tips to break the perfectionism cycle, developed with Dr. Hart:

   IDENTIFY PERFECTIONISTIC THINKING.
   - **If/then:** If I get it "perfect," then I will be _____ (happy, loved, accepted, good enough, appreciated, etc.).
   - **Comparing:** How might I be holding myself to an unrealistic standard? Who am I comparing myself to? Do I find myself asking, "Why can't I do as well as others?"

- **Self-judgment:** What are some of the self-critical thoughts that I have about my own abilities? Begin to notice and label judgments and negative self-talk.

ADJUST EXPECTATIONS.

- **Shift self-evaluations** away from the result (*i.e.*, what I have or haven't accomplished) toward the process (*i.e.*, the learning and growth that I might experience along the way).
- **Set healthy boundaries** with yourself: Instead of thinking you must do it all, think about what you really want, rather than what you think you *should* want.
- **Set achievable goals** and reward yourself for meeting them—allow yourself to set a new goal or "re-goal" if that first goal is not realistic. No need to abandon your effort altogether.

MAKE MISTAKES! LOVE AND EMBRACE THEM.

- **Embrace the process of trial and error!** Mistakes are an essential part of growth, and they can be some of our greatest teachers and lessons. Remember that there is not one single "right" way to accomplish a given task.

REMEMBER SELF-COMPASSION.

- **Common humanity:** You likely accept that no one is perfect. How can you recognize and accept your own humanity as you would another person's?
- **Self-kindness:** How can you replace self-judgment with self-kindness and patience, treating yourself and talking to yourself like you would treat or talk to a dear friend?
- **Mindfulness:** How can you step outside of yourself and *be with* yourself and your experience, rather than being stuck in the perfectionism trap of reward and punishment?

3. Set flexible standards instead of hard-and-fast rules:

Think about the last time you felt like you "failed" at something. What happened? What made you think that you failed? Was there an expectation that you set for yourself (or that someone else set for you) that you were not able to meet? What was the outcome? Was there a reward or punishment?

Identify the Expectation:

If _____, then _____
_____.

Now rewrite the expectation as a flexible standard:

_____

_____

_____

Note: Ditching perfect and embracing more flexible standards does not mean settling for mediocrity—rather, it means broadly shifting more of our focus from *outcome* to *process*, the *how we are doing* to the *what we are doing*, and enabling ourselves to learn and grow, through what may even feel like failure.

## CHAPTER 4

# Explore

Overcoming our deepest fears and not letting them hold us back from moving in our desired direction in life is an important step toward self-actualization. But it is only part of the journey. While the base of security is safety, the base of growth is *exploration*. To use our sailboat metaphor, we can make sure the boat is secure and stable, but until we fully open the sails and move in the vast unknown of the sea amid the inevitable winds and waves, we are unlikely to grow to our fullest capacities.

The need for exploration—the desire to seek out and make sense of the world, in all its novelty, challenge, and uncertainty, is an irreducible part of the human experience.[1] This need has many different manifestations, including learning about and from other people, mastering novel or complex adventures, making meaning from trauma and challenges, and using one's imagination, intellectual curiosity, and creative thinking to explore the depths of our own minds.

You can gauge your own need to explore by examining the following five statements in a scale created by psychologist Todd Kashdan and his colleagues.

EXPLORATION SCALE[2]
- ❏ I view challenging situations as an opportunity to grow and learn.
- ❏ I am always looking for experiences that challenge how I think about myself and the world.

❑ I seek out situations where it is likely that I will have to think in depth about something.

❑ I enjoy learning about subjects that are unfamiliar to me.

❑ I find it fascinating to learn new information.

Kashdan and his colleagues found that folks scoring higher on the need for exploration tend to have higher "stress tolerance," defined as the willingness to embrace the inherent anxiety of new, complex, mysterious, unexpected, and obscure events. Stress tolerance is strongly correlated with happiness, meaning in life, autonomy, relatedness, and the presence of positive emotions. It is also required to genuinely expand beyond the confines of our comfort zones.

In the rest of this chapter, we will traverse the boundaries of our comfort zones, explore the totality of ourselves (even the "darkest" parts), and practice ways to deconstruct some of the defenses we place between ourselves and the world around us through social exploration, meaning-making, humor, and creativity.

# EXPAND YOUR COMFORT ZONE

My comfort zone is like a little bubble around me,
and I've pushed it in different directions and made it bigger and bigger
until these objectives that seemed totally crazy,
eventually fall within the realm of the possible.
—Alex Honnold, world-renowned free solo climber

In service of our own growth and need for exploration, many of us would likely benefit from expanding the boundaries of our comfort zones. Having a comfort zone is not inherently a bad thing, especially in our modern world, in which even some of the most basic activities of daily life—going to the gym, work, or the grocery store, or even socializing with friends—have been transformed into real questions of safety versus threat.

However, when we confine ourselves to our psychological comfort zones, we may develop a pattern of avoiding situations that bring up potentially undesirable internal bodily states, emotions, thoughts, memories, or behaviors. As a result, we may deprive ourselves of fully engaging with life and experiencing critical parts of our human experience. Avoidance of undesirable feelings is a phenomenon that psychologist Dr. Steven Hayes, the father of Acceptance and Commitment Therapy (ACT), calls "experiential avoidance."[3] Indeed, experiential avoidance is a profound barrier to exploration, and learning to manage it is a central theme of modern behavioral therapies, including ACT, Dialectical Behavioral Therapy (DBT), Cognitive Behavioral Therapy (CBT), and others.

An antidote to avoidance is what Hayes calls "psychological flexibility," a process of welcoming discomfort and the internal experiences that arise in response to a given situation with openness and nonjudgment. We can all cultivate the ability to engage with whatever the present moment brings, without needless defense, and, depending on the situation, persist or alter our behaviors in the pursuit of our highest values and goals.[4]

Psychological flexibility is closely related to mindfulness—which expert Cory Muscara defines as the process of being *with* our experience,[5] curiously, openly, and nonjudgmentally. Research indicates that both mindfulness and psychological flexibility together uniquely predict long-term functioning and quality of life, after even the strongest forms of trauma.[6]

So, how can we cultivate and nurture our inherent capacity for exploration, enhance our stress tolerance and psychological flexibility, and mindfully expand the bounds of our comfort zones (or even transcend them)? In the most general terms, we can practice *welcoming*, rather than avoiding, stressful situations and practice leaning in to potentially uncomfortable internal experiences, and accepting whatever emotions, thoughts, and physical sensations arise.

Then, when discomfort inevitably sets in, rather than try to minimize or fight the negative experiences, we practice sitting with them, bringing a sense of curiosity to the experience, and using our personal values and goals as a compass to guide how we act.

## PRACTICE

1. Spend some time reflecting on what comes up for you when you think about the boundaries of your own psychological comfort zone. You may even find it helpful to draw a picture of your comfort zone and fill in what sorts of things fall within the confines and outside of the confines of your comfort zone at this moment.

2. Reflect on the following questions:
   - How have the boundaries of my comfort zone helped me to feel safe and secure recently, throughout the pandemic and in other aspects of my life?
   - What measures have I taken to preserve my comfort zone?
   - What are the primary emotions that I feel when I am in my comfort zone? What does my body feel like when I am in my comfort zone? What thoughts come up when I think about remaining in my comfort zone?
   - What emotions, bodily sensations, and thoughts arise when I think about stepping outside of my comfort zone?
     - Cue for psychological flexibility and stress-tolerance: How might I welcome any of these potentially uncomfortable or difficult sensations and just be with them, without judgment?

- How have the confines of my comfort zone shape-shifted or changed throughout my life? In what ways has my comfort zone expanded or contracted with my life experiences?

3. After reflecting on these questions, consider setting yourself up for an experience doing something that makes you feel *uncomfortable* and brings you outside of your current psychological comfort zone. *Please do not choose to do anything that is objectively unsafe or traverse solo into an area rife with unprocessed trauma without the guidance of a trained mental health professional.*

Consider the following ideas to help you get started. As you read our suggestions, worthy contenders are those that may initially bring about some feelings of doubt or even anxiety within you and feel like a bit of a stretch, but that don't feel entirely out of the realm of possibility.

- Set out to formally learn about a new topic that is currently unknown to you, or perhaps that you are skeptical about.
- Convene a conversation about a challenging topic on which you hold firm views, inviting folks with all different points of view, including those who oppose you (and vow to listen, *really listen*, and learn something new).
- Plan a trip to a new place that is totally unfamiliar to you and spend time learning about the customs and culture of this place.
- Start a conversation with a total stranger in a public place.
- Say "yes" to the next spontaneous idea that a friend has for you.
- Cleanse from technology! Unplug from all electronics—including your cellphone and all messaging apps—for a full day (start with twelve hours and up-titrate to a full twenty-four!).

If you tend to be more introverted . . .

- Reach out to someone you have been wanting to make a connection with but have found an excuse not to.

- Ask someone out on a date (be it a friend date or a romantic date).
- Host a dinner party, bringing together people from different walks of your life.
- Attend a new event in your community, such as an art show or a workout class. Stir up conversation with someone new.

If you tend to be more social and extraverted . . .

- Go out for a meal, movie, or show alone!
- Spend an entire weekend in solitude.
- Plan a solo vacation and travel to a new place all by yourself.

Whatever you choose, the goal should be to try something new: to expand the boundaries of what you're currently comfortable with. While completing this activity, allow yourself to lean in to all the feelings that arise. Expect that it will likely feel uncomfortable at times. Try to understand what physical sensations you experience in real time, and what things you can do to welcome, rather than suppress or try to minimize, unpleasant sensations, such as confusion, fear, and anxiety.

4. After completing the activity, reflect on the following questions:
   - What went well for me?
   - What was the most challenging part of the experience?
   - What, if anything, did I learn about myself?
   - How might pushing the bounds of my existing comfort zone inform my sense of competence, possibility, and growth for the future?

Don't stop here—continue to practice accepting and being with the totality of your experience as you traverse the boundaries of your comfort zone in daily life. Deliberately cross these bounds and check in with yourself to identify how the boundaries of your comfort zone morph over time.

# BE SOCIALLY CURIOUS

This growth challenge is about cultivating social curiosity to see the people in our lives for who they really are, rather than who we want them to be.

## PRACTICE

1. Choose someone in your life with whom you will practice your social curiosity. This can be someone you know very well, or it can be someone with whom you have a newer relationship (and it can certainly be done in "real life" or through electronic means). The next time you engage with this person, try to learn or notice something about them that you never knew before. You can start out subtly, by just paying more attention to their expressions, their smile, their voice, etc.

2. When you feel comfortable, start to ask questions that demonstrate your interest in this person. Be sure to use your judgment about when showing this curiosity is appropriate, and be ready to reciprocate and allow your partner to ask questions as well. Some question suggestions might include the following (see the "Small Talk, Big Talk" questions in chapter 2 for more ideas).
   • What would your perfect day entail?
   • If you could share a meal with anyone in the world, dead or alive, who would it be and why?
   • What would others say is your greatest strength, and why?
   • What is your biggest fear?
   • What is a dream you have for the near future? For the distant future?
   • Where do you see yourself in the next five years, ten years?

3. Reflect on what you notice about the quality of your connection with this person.

4. Write a written reflection about the experience of pursuing social curiosity, what came of this exercise, and anything else that you might have learned.

---

# EXPLORE YOUR DARK SIDE

Do I contradict myself?
Very well, then I contradict myself,
(I am large, I contain multitudes).
—Walt Whitman, *Song of Myself*

There is so much complexity within human nature and the human psyche; within all of us, there is not just a single self, but a bundle of various and sometimes conflicting impulses, emotions, roles, and drives. The great humanistic psychotherapist Rollo May argued that virtually all humans "are bundles of both evil and good potentialities."[7] Integrating these parts of ourselves can result in tremendous creativity and growth, whereas complete disintegration can result in destruction—both to oneself and to others.

Carl Rogers—another great humanistic psychotherapist—wrote that a common fear among his patients was that therapy would "release the beast" within themselves if they became too accepting of their "dark sides" and leaned in to previously unknown or suppressed aspects of themselves.[8] However, Rogers found that actually the opposite was true: fully open self-analysis and self-exploration enabled people to strike a more effective and productive balance of honoring both the light and the dark within them. Rogers believed that it is only when we deny awareness of various aspects of our experience that we have reason to fear them. Accordingly, one is most fully human or "fully functioning" when one's various experiences of being human—the good, the bad, the ugly, the beautiful—operate in a sort of constructive harmony.[9]

For instance, feelings like guilt, anger, or embarrassment, when acknowledged, can serve as emotional cues that we may find utility in repenting, resolving a conflict, or learning to do something differently next time.[10] The experience of anxiety may feel intensely distressing in our minds and bodies; and it may simply be viewed as a cue that we are feeling threatened in some way, and we can embrace and "thank" our anxiety for warning us of potential dangers (whether these are real or simply imagined). The point is, instead of shoving these unpleasant experiences below our level of consciousness, tucking them away in a metaphorical box we hide under our beds, we can welcome them to a seat at our proverbial kitchen table, thank them for working to ensure our survival, and then tell them, "I actually don't need you right now." It is when we choose to embrace, rather than suppress, such experiences in our lives that we can adequately respond to and integrate them.

Similarly, features of our lives that may sometimes feel to us like "scars," such as struggling with physical or mental illness, harboring a particular insecurity, or experiencing tragedy or trauma, when acknowledged and welcomed into our lives can, with time, become sources of strength, connection, and growth. For example, experiencing even the most catastrophic life events, such as losing our loved ones or livelihoods, or other forms of personal or collective adversity, can serve as catalysts for growth, *e.g.*, renewed appreciation of life, a greater connection with another person, or a renewed sense of spirituality.[11]

Interestingly, this path to growth is not necessarily automatic and often requires a great deal of processing and pain along the way. This, too, we may welcome. Ultimately, it may require opening ourselves to hostility, aggression, and anger that can accompany confronting these emotions directly. When we suppress (consciously) or repress (unconsciously) our darkest thoughts, these may find their way to "erupt" into our lives, like a volcano, when we are not prepared, frequently with grave consequences.[12]

This practice involves safely reexperiencing and confronting some of our own dark emotions, impulses, and negative experiences, and deliberately unlocking the potential for growth that they might unleash.

## PRACTICE

1. Spend some time in a quiet place reflecting on what your "dark side" means to you. You may use some or all of the following questions to guide you:
   - What comes to mind when thinking about my dark side?
   - What, if any, parts of myself do I keep to myself, hide from others, or tend to wish I could tuck away and keep in a box hidden below my bed?
   - What, if any, situation(s) in my life consistently bring forth uncomfortable emotions (*e.g.*, guilt, anger, sadness, loneliness, frustration) for me?
   - What do I personally struggle with the most that I might consider a "scar"?

Of course, you can repeat this exercise as many times as you wish, but start by choosing one dimension of your dark side to engage with for now. Perhaps begin with something that is not *too raw* or sensitive for you in this moment and that feels accessible to engage with without unraveling.

2. Really lean in to this facet of your dark side. Embody the emotion, experience, situation, or scar. Sit with it for a few moments and breathe it into your body. Say "welcome" and imagine that you are inviting this part of yourself to sit with you at your table. (If it helps, consider giving this piece of yourself a name, to help personify and humanize it. Allow this to be a kind, rather than a degrading, name.)

3. Reflect on what it feels like to let our dark side in—to willingly allow it to join us at a time of our choosing.
   - How does it feel for me to open the door to this part of myself?
   - How can I offer this part of myself tenderness and care? What might I say to this part of myself?

- How has my dark side strengthened me?
- How might this part of myself help me connect more deeply with other people?

4. Now, how might I set a *healthy boundary* with this part of myself? How can I invite this part of myself into my life in appropriate doses in appropriate settings (*i.e.*, inviting it in for lunch on Tuesday instead of for an extended, open-ended stay, or expelling it from my home completely)?

The next time you feel tempted to suppress this part of yourself, perhaps play with welcoming it in at planned times, entertaining it for a few minutes, and then opening the door to let it go on its way.

## EMBRACE POST-TRAUMATIC GROWTH

A core feature of fostering growth in the aftermath of trauma is transforming "intrusive ruminations"—the experience of being flooded with negative thoughts about an experience, often in inappropriate times and settings—into "deliberate rumination." Deliberate rumination involves consciously and willingly choosing when and how we process the details of a difficult experience in a well-boundaried, thoughtful way. So how do we reconstruct unpleasant, intrusive ruminations, such as nightmares, "daymares," or unsettling flashbacks, into content that we engage with head-on, on our own terms?

For one, we can journal about our challenges, engaging with ourselves and our own internal dialogues and narratives. Really, this entire book is geared toward doing just this! We can also talk to others, friends and confidants, or professional counselors or therapists, about these experiences. Just as we practiced in the previous exercise, we can also carve out specific time to write, think, and talk about such challenges, as to create a semi-permeable container for them without shutting them out completely. Yes, we can literally schedule worry time into our day! Importantly, we can also explicitly reflect on the doors that have opened for us, and that may open for us in the future, not despite, but *because* of, our adversity.

## PRACTICE

1. Think about a time in the past when you personally faced a significant adversity or loss. First, write and reflect about the doors that closed due to that adversity/loss.
   - What did I lose?
   - How did it feel in the moment?
   - How does it feel now?

2. Next, write about any potential doors that opened in the aftermath of that adversity/ loss. While you would have never asked for this adversity or loss to occur, what do you take with you from that in your life today that might be viewed as positive?
   - Are there any new ways of acting, thinking, or relating to others or to myself that have become more accessible now?
   - What, if anything, have I learned from this experience that will inform the way I move into the future?

3. If relevant, consider a significant adversity or loss that is still raw for you now.
   - In what ways is this adversity showing up in my life right now? How might it be intruding on me or popping up unwittingly?
   - How am I already addressing this deliberately and taking steps to process the experience? If these are working for me, how might I do more of this? If these steps are not working for me, what else might I do?
   - What might I learn from my past experiences of loss or adversity that might help me process this experience?
   - What might this experience feel like one year from now? Five years from now?

# EMBRACE THE ABSURD

Humor is one of the greatest tools that we have at our disposal to explore and cope with the often dark and absurd world around us and connect with others. In fact, in George

Vaillant's famous seventy-five-year Harvard study, he uncovered that our ability to use humor—specifically for good, rather than at the expense of others—is associated with greater growth, healthy adaptation to life, positive mental health, warm human relationships, and successful careers.[13] Humor, he says, "is one of the truly elegant defenses in the human repertoire . . . The capacity for humor, like hope, is one of man's most potent antidotes for the woes of Pandora's box."[14] Indeed, a good sense of humor is something to be taken very seriously!

Beyond just a defense to protect us from the woes of the world, humor is a transcendent character strength, a positive emotion, an ingredient in healthy and high-functioning workplaces and schools, and a fierce driver of positive relationships. Research reveals that humor helps foster positive learning environments and relationships among teachers and their students and helps school-age children learn complex concepts and retain material.[15] It is also a powerful tool for increasing psychotherapy patients' willingness to change attitudes and behaviors.[16] Not to mention, humor is a highly socially attractive trait frequently prioritized in friends and in partner selection![17]

While humor may be defined in many ways and has no single agreed-upon definition in the psychological literature, we think about humor as the ability to appreciate and enjoy the idiosyncrasies of life, to laugh and make others laugh, and to see the funny side of otherwise painful situations.

This simple practice is about explicitly nurturing our sense of humor to seek and embrace what is hilarious, ridiculous, amusing, and comical about our daily lives. Researchers have found that folks who engage in this type of practice experience increased levels of happiness at one- and three-month follow-ups, and amelioration of depressive symptoms up to six months later.[18]

## PRACTICE

1. For seven consecutive days, spend time each evening writing down three funny things that you came across during the day. You can write about times you laughed throughout the day, a joke you might have heard, a funny video you came across, a

particularly joyful interaction, or an instance when you laughed at yourself or sought humor under stress.

Write down the feelings you had during each experience. How did these moments shape the tone of your day? Did you share these moments with others? Reflect on the details.

Bonus points if you complete this practice with someone else in your life. Consider sharing one of your funny things and spread the humor! (Remember, when it comes to funny things, sometimes, you really do have to be there!)

2. After this weeklong practice, see how you feel. What types of humorous situations showed up most? Do you tend to notice more humorous or absurd things happening during the day in real time? Consider continuing this practice beyond one week.

3. Reflect on how you might bring humor into more of what you do during the day. For example, how might you share moments of humor with loved ones, over dinner, or at the start of a work meeting?

## OPEN YOUR MIND

Creativity has its roots in the nonrational . . .
Science and education, being too exclusively abstract, verbal
and bookish, do not have enough place for raw, concrete, esthetic
experience, especially of the subjective happenings inside oneself.
—Abraham Maslow, *Toward a Psychology of Being*

As we've now delved into several facets of exploration, including learning about and from other people, embarking on adventures to expand our comfort zones, embracing the totality of our human experiences, making meaning from trauma and challenges, and using our sense of humor, let's dive into our intellectual curiosity and creativity. Of all the personality traits a person can have, the trait that is most consistently associated with creativity is *openness to experience*.[19] Openness to experience may be thought of as the drive for cognitive exploration of one's experience. Take a look at the Openness to Experience Scale and see how much you agree with each form of cognitive exploration that psychologists have discovered:

OPENNESS TO EXPERIENCE SCALE

❑ I am fascinated by art, music, or literature.

❑ I see beauty in things others might not notice.

❑ I enjoy imagining things vividly.

❑ Sometimes I am so immersed in nature or in art that I feel as if my whole state of consciousness has somehow been temporarily changed.

❑ When I have a strong emotional experience, the effect stays with me for a long time.

❑ I often lose awareness of time and my physical surroundings.

❑ There is often a sense of "closeness" to what I am creating, a greater-than-normal emotional connection with it.

❑ I am curious about many different things.

❑ I am inventive and find clever ways to do things.

❑ I am original and come up with new ideas.

❑ I enjoy intellectual challenges.

❑ I seek out situations that require thinking in depth about something.

❑ I don't like to know the answer without understanding the reasoning behind it.

Taken together, the full richness of the openness-to-experience domain provides the seeds for creative thinking and creative behavior. While not everyone has the capacity, will, or resources to become a Leonardo da Vinci, we are all wired for creativity.[20] Creativity is like a muscle: You use it or lose it. The best way to jog your creativity is by increasing the habits of openness and repeating them over and over as your default way of being. To help you with that, consider the following:

• When was the last time I engaged in a creative pursuit, such as those in the scale above?

- When was the last time I made space for myself to just daydream about my hopes and desires, and nothing more?

The late "father of daydreaming," psychologist Jerome L. Singer (and a significant mentor of Scott's), referred to "positive-constructive daydreaming" as playful, wishful imagery and linked it to creative thought.[21] Critically, he differentiated this form of daydreaming from the inability to control one's attention and from the presence of intrusive guilty and dysphoric thoughts. Additionally, the great creativity researcher E. Paul Torrance wrote that "one of the most powerful wellsprings of creative energy, outstanding accomplishment, and self-fulfillment seems to be falling in love with something—your dreams, your image of the future."[22]

## PRACTICE

1. **Daydream.** Take a quiet spot, close your eyes, and allow yourself to begin some "positive-constructive daydreaming." Spend some time cultivating an image of a *version of you* that you may have never thought possible—an image of yourself in the future that you particularly like but never dared to imagine or express before. Remove as many distractions as possible, pouring forth your entire being into this task—come what may. You can always error-correct later, but for the moment allow your mind, body, and full awareness to penetrate the depth of the experience. Put your full consciousness on the task of imagining this possible you; treat it as though it were the only thing that exists in the entire world and for all time.

2. **Get creative.** After you've immersed yourself in this image, set out to deeply engage in a creative activity. Use the reflection of your image of the future to guide your creative pursuit and unlock your creative potential. Perhaps you are compelled to plan a trip, cook a delicious feast, read a particular form of literature, write a poem, visit an art museum, go for a hike in nature, listen to an album that moves you, produce a piece of art, or seek beauty in something you have seen many times. Whatever you choose to do, bring forth your full awareness and go all in.

3. **Reflect on the creative experience.** When you complete the daydreaming-creativity sequence, reflect on what the process felt like: What did it feel like to stretch your creativity muscles through imagery and a more active creative pursuit? What does this activate inside of you? How might you bring more creativity into your daily life?

4. **Get intellectually curious.** Another major dimension of cognitive exploration is *intellectual curiosity*. The next time someone gives you their opinion about something or you read a news headline, take a moment to reflect on it from various angles. Treat what they are saying with great curiosity. What's the evidence for what they are saying? What would the evidence have to look like for what they are saying to be true? What evidence would disprove their opinion? How might you have thought about the situation incorrectly in the past? What blinders do you have on that might be preventing you from seeing the truth?

## CHAPTER 5

# Love

Love is the only sane and satisfactory answer
to the problem of human existence.
—Erich Fromm, *The Art of Loving*

We live in a time of great division. We are all so attached to our own group identities that it may be difficult for us to find the common humanity with someone who has a very different worldview than we have. Is there a higher form of love that can transcend our human tendency for tribalism? Can we possibly love people we don't even *like* very much? We think so.

We like to distinguish between the need for connection and the need for love. We already covered the immense benefits of feeling as though we belong and having intimate relationships with at least a few people in our lives. Psychological research also shows the immense benefits of giving love unconditionally. In his book *Spiritual Evolution*, the psychiatrist George Vaillant writes that "successful human development involves, first, absorbing love, next, reciprocally sharing love, and finally, giving love unselfishly away."[1] We can give love even when we don't feel an immediate connection with someone, and even when we don't obviously connect over a common group identity.

In her book *Real Love: The Art of Mindful Connection*, Buddhist meditation teacher Sharon Salzberg discusses her idea of "real love," which she defines as the innate capacity we all possess to love, in which love is a freely given gift. She says that we all have deep reservoirs of love within us that we can tap into anytime to generate even more love in our lives.[2] Related to this idea, the humanistic philosopher Erich Fromm writes about mature love, which is an active process, an attitude more than a feeling.[3] As a person matures, and the needs of others become just as important as the needs of one's self, a person gradually transforms the idea of love from "being loved" into "loving," from a state of dependency in which one is rewarded by being loved to a loving orientation in which one is capable of loving the world at large.

Psychological research confirms that the need for "beneficence"—being able to give to others—improves well-being, and that this need may not be completely reducible to other needs such as connection, competence, and autonomy.[4] Beneficence does not just involve wanting to give to others within our own in-group, either, but wanting to give to all people, an idea called *universalism*. There are many ways to flex the need for love, from volunteering, to everyday acts of kindness, to spending money on others.[5] Research around the world has even shown that giving anonymously can increase the feelings of beneficence (the "warm glow of giving"[6]), as well as well-being.[7] It seems humans have a built-in pro-social drive that propels us to help others and in which we feel rewarded for doing so.[8]

Scott's research with his colleagues on the "light triad" shows that having a beneficent orientation toward others can be cultivated as a *way of being*.[9] We place too much of a premium in our society on doing and often underestimate the value of being. This applies to the need for love. Giving as a strategy *in the service of personal gain over others* is not the same as constantly uplifting others just by being who we are and showing up kindly in our daily interactions with others.[10]

The three main elements of the light triad—*Kantianism* (treating people as ends unto themselves, rather than as means to other ends), *humanism* (valuing the dignity and worth of each individual), and *faith in humanity* (believing in the fundamental goodness of humans)—have been linked to genuine motives for helping others and a wide range of growth-oriented outcomes, such as increased connection with others, life satisfaction, and higher levels of curiosity and exploration.[11] In this chapter we will give you some exercises to help you flex your love muscles and connect with the humanity of others, regardless of how much we immediately or naturally connect with them.

# GIVE

Giving our time, openly and without expectation of receiving anything in return, is one of the greatest acts of love that we can put into the world. Naturally motivated acts of philanthropy and altruism have been widely studied to produce physical and psychological benefits, including decreased rates of depression and lower blood pressure and enhanced life satisfaction and longevity.[12] Even relatively brief acts of kindness, including those that are assigned or prescribed, such as a ninety-minute "pay it forward" intervention where individuals who received kindness were implored to carry kindness forward toward others, have been shown to enhance optimism, gratitude, life satisfaction, and joviality among givers.[13] During the pandemic, even simply reflecting on acts of kindness has been shown to enhance positive emotions among research participants.[14]

## PRACTICE

1. Spend some time reflecting on acts of kindness that you have engaged in for other people, as well as some meaningful acts of kindness that you have received from others. Make a list of at least five kind things you have done for other people this week, and five things you have received from others this week.

| ACTS OF KINDNESS I DID FOR OTHERS | ACTS OF KINDNESS OTHERS DID FOR ME |
|---|---|
| 1. | 1. |
| 2. | 2. |
| 3. | 3. |
| 4. | 4. |
| 5. | 5. |

2. Zoom in on one of these acts on your list that you did for someone else this week. Write about this act in detail. What did I do? What motivated me to do this behavior? How did the other person react?

3. Set yourself up for more. This week, deliberately engage in at least five acts of virtue or kindness for another person (a partner, friend, colleague, boss, mentor, stranger, etc.). These do not need to be for the same person, and the person does not need to be aware of the act. Try to mix and vary the types of kindness activities you perform, and, if possible, try to chunk them together between one or two days, rather than sprinkling them throughout the week, as research shows that chunking good deeds shows greater psychological benefits to the giver.[15]

Anonymous acts can include simple gestures, like washing someone else's dishes, picking up litter on the street, making an anonymous donation, or leaving chocolate on a colleague's desk. More relational acts of kindness can include helping a neighbor with work at home, giving your time to help a friend with errands, cooking a meal for friends, visiting or calling a relative, or volunteering for a charity or philanthropic organization. At the end of each activity, reflect on your acts by writing them down with the date of completion and exactly what you did.

| ACTS OF KINDNESS LOG | |
| --- | --- |
| DATE | ACTIVITY |
| | 1. |
| | 2. |
| | 3. |
| | 4. |
| | 5. |

At the end of the five activities, reflect on your log. Did any of your acts of kindness bring you closer to other people? How did these acts make you feel? How did they make others feel? Did any stand out relative to the others?

Did any of your acts of kindness proliferate other acts of kindness, either within yourself or for others?

# THE STATUE OF DAVID AND YOU

Have you ever noticed that the "version of yourself" that you portray in the presence of others often looks and feels quite different, depending on the company you're in? Perhaps you have a very close friend, romantic partner, or colleague who seems to bring out characteristics in you that you cherish and love about yourself, such as silliness, curiosity, or confidence. In these cases, your partner is likely communicating to you— be it directly or indirectly, consciously or unconsciously, and through words or actions—that they see you and support these qualities in you that you cherish. On the other hand, you may also have relationships with people who communicate indifference, pessimism, or disapproval of these same characteristics.[16] In the company of this person, you may find yourself manifesting qualities that you quite dislike about yourself, perhaps feeling irritable, on edge, or defensive.

Our movement toward our own "ideal selves," or the constellation of traits, skills, and resources that make up our dreams and aspirations for ourselves[17] (and which certainly may change over the course of our lives), is actually a deeply *interpersonal* process that others may help "sculpt" from within us. Just as Michelangelo Buonarroti, the Renaissance sculptor, painter, and master artist, chiseled, carved, and polished his *David* from a slab of marble, revealing his ideal form from within, so too are our ideal selves revealed when those we are closest to affirm us. This process has been termed the *Michelangelo phenomenon* and has been validated by robust psychological research.

One study of married partners who were videotaped discussing goals relevant to each person's ideal self found that those whose partners exhibited affirming behaviors such as clarifying plans, offering assistance, or praising their partner's goal pursuits were more likely to achieve their ideal-self goals four months later.[18]

The theory also discusses the importance of moving beyond simply understanding and encouraging our partner's ideals. Researchers behind the Michelangelo phenomenon, Caryl Rusbult, Eli Finkel, and Madoka Kumashiro, assert that to sculpt our partner's ideal self most effectively from the proverbial block of stone, we must understand not just the "ideal form slumbering within the block," but we must also understand the block itself: the possibilities and potential flaws that must be circumvented. In other words, we must meet our partners where they are, supporting their actual perceptions of themselves[19] in service of and in addition to promoting the best within them.

These researchers also urge that we must avoid a common pitfall called the *Pygmalion phenomenon*, or the tendency to perceive and behave toward our partners in ways consistent with our own, but not our partner's, ideal self. We may fall into this trap when we believe that we know best what is best for our partner and project our own ideal-self representation onto them. This has been shown to undercut both personal and couple well-being. An antidote to this Pygmalion phenomenon is what humanistic psychologist Carl Rogers referred to as "unconditional positive regard" (see the Embrace High-Quality Connections practice in chapter 2). When we accept and view others warmly, with genuine care, as their own person, we give them "full permission to have their own feelings" and "their own experiences."[20]

Let's practice embracing the Michelangelo phenomenon with another person in our lives, and work toward the lifelong process of becoming masterpieces together.

## PRACTICE

First, find a partner who you will engage in this practice. This will ideally be someone you consider an integral part of your life, such as a romantic partner, a dear friend, a family member, a roommate, or a close work colleague. Invite your partner to read the above text to understand the Michelangelo phenomenon and the Pygmalion phenomenon before diving in.

**1. Reflect on the current state of your own block of stone, and the statue lying dormant within.**

Allow each partner to spend a few moments quietly reflecting on the following questions. Write down your answers.

- What does my "ideal self" mean to me right now? What are some of the hopes and goals that I am working toward? What qualities, skills, and resources do I aspire to possess?
- Where am I right now in relation to my ideal self? What qualities, skills, and resources do I possess right now that might help facilitate my goal attainment? What are some potential barriers that I see myself facing in pursuit of my goal(s)? What qualities, skills, and resources might be required for me to attain these goals that I may not already possess?

**2. Share your reflections with your partner.**

Be fully present with one another as you listen to your partner's hopes and vision for their ideal self. Take in what you hear about where each of you are now and where you hope to be. Refrain from trying to convince your partner that they are already further along toward their ideal self than they are. Also refrain from passing any judgment or lukewarm enthusiasm. Just try to meet them wherever they are with unconditional openness and validation. Thank one another for sharing.

**3. Sharpen your tools.**

Spend some time back in quiet reflection mode, thinking about what behaviors you might exhibit to help chisel, carve, and polish your partner's ideal form from their block of stone. How might you help support the vision that your partner has for themself?

**4. Share your ideas with your partner and ask for feedback.**

Discuss these ideas with your partner, asking, "Would it be helpful for you if I _____ in support of your goal?" Engage in dialogue to help refine the helping behaviors in a way that your partner would find most effective. You can of course ask one another for suggestions as well.

**5. Commit and follow up.**
Commit to these behaviors to help manifest the ideal self of your partner. Remember, this is about *their ideals for themselves, not your ideals for them*. Decide on a time when you can check in with one another about how this process is going and refine as needed.

# LOVE YOUR ENEMIES

Political divisiveness is bad for the country, our shared well-being, and our personal happiness. As professor, social scientist, and author of *Love Your Enemies: How Decent People Can Save America from the Culture of Contempt*, Arthur Brooks puts it:

> *In our politics today, the biggest threat we face is rejecting kindness not in favor of anger, but of contempt. As we have seen, contempt destroys unity and leads to permanent division. It's the political equivalent of using a weapon of mass destruction. In an arms race, it sometimes feels as though one must adopt this weapon. That is incorrect. In the long run, niceness and strength (with occasional righteous anger) are the right combination for effective, authoritative leadership and the best way to win—because in the long run, people are instinctively attracted to happy warriors who fight for others.*[21]

In an experiment designed to test openness to political opinions, researchers found that 62 percent of Americans would forgo being paid $3 to avoid hearing from the other side.[22] The study found that both politically liberal and conservative individuals were highly motivated to avoid hearing one another's opinions, assuming that doing so would result in anger and division. This practice is designed to implement psychological tools to help us lower the level of discomfort we feel when hearing from people with whom we disagree. Written by experts Arthur Brooks and Reece Brown, this practice deploys three methods derived from findings in psychology and neuroscience:

1. Practicing intimacy melds us with others and creates empathy and understanding.

2. Increasing our knowledge of others breaks down faulty assumptions that others have hateful intentions.

3. Kindness and expressed gratitude are psychological superpowers that each of us can use to physiologically raise well-being in our lives and the lives of others.

If we want more unity, less contempt, and more universal love, Brooks writes, "We need to get out of our comfort zones, go where we are not welcome, and spend time talking and interacting with people with whom we disagree—not on lightweight stuff like sports and food, but on hard moral things."

Research shows that people tend to exaggerate the degree of difference between themselves and people on the other political side. This perpetuates what psychological scientists call "motive attribution asymmetry," or the tendency to believe that our own motives are based in love and our opponent's are based in hate.[23] This exercise is built to counteract this asymmetry through greater curiosity, knowledge, empathy, and compassion.

## PRACTICE

First, find a partner for this experiment, ideally someone with whom you disagree politically. It could be a close friend, a colleague, or a neighbor; just make sure you know they don't hold all of the same views as you. Next, find a few sheets of paper and something to write with.

### 1. Get to know your partner.

As we've explored in chapter 2, psychologist Arthur Aron has shown in the lab that having two individuals ask a series of increasingly personal questions leads to feelings of closeness.[24] The first step in the exercise builds on that work. Ask each other the following five questions:

- Where do you feel most at home?
- What is your happiest memory?
- What keeps you up at night?
- What is the best example of people working together you have seen or experienced?
- If you were given the power to eliminate suffering, how would you use it?

### 2. Build your knowledge.

- Make two lists: write down the five things most important to you in your life, and the five things you believe are most important to your political other.
- Put aside the list you wrote for yourself and hold the list you wrote based on your guesses about the other person's top five items.
- Give the list you wrote about yourself to the other person.
- Exchange the lists that you each wrote for each other. Where were you mistaken? What items do you have in common?
- Tell the other person what you learned about them from their list, especially what surprised you. Discuss any expectations you had that were wrong, such as the priorities you thought the other person had that turned out to be inaccurate.

### 3. Compliment and thank.

We expect to be judged harshly by others in social situations, which is why we refrain from giving compliments. But research finds that compliment-givers consistently underestimate the positive impact of their compliment to its recipient and that they overestimate how bothered the person is by being approached.[25] Even in cases between complete strangers, the stigma of awkwardness is hugely misprescribed compared to the emotional benefit to the compliment receiver and giver. In addition, expressing gratitude raises our positive emotions and creates bonds with the receiver of the thanks.[26]

- Say thank you to your partner for their time, attention, and willingness to do the exercise with you! Compliment them on something that genuinely impressed you—even if it's just their sneakers!

## BEING LOVE

This exercise is about opening our hearts and minds to a kinder, more compassionate view of others and the self, so that we may move toward greater equanimity with ourselves and our world.

## PRACTICE

Use the space below as a contemplative, meditative opportunity to reflect as you move through this practice. Feel free to take notes or jot down reflections as you go, if that feels helpful to you.

1. Bring to mind someone in your life who it is relatively easy for you to love. This can be someone who brightens your day, someone you would call for help if you needed them, or someone who understands you and sees you in a way that you want to be seen. Write down their name.
   - In your mind's eye, cultivate their image. *Imagine that they are smiling at you. Perhaps you imagine what it is like to be physically in their presence, to share a cup of tea, to laugh together, to embrace.* What emotions arise for you? What sensations do you feel in your body?
   - Next, imagine sending this person a blessing that feels genuine to you. Feel free to come up with your own loving blessing. If you prefer, you may use or modify this one:

*May you be safe. May you be protected from harm and feel a sense of ease. May you find strength and wisdom in the challenges that life has thrown at you. May you feel supported and unafraid. May you know how much I care about you.*

- Reflect on how you feel sending this blessing toward your loved one.
  - Have you shared these sentiments with this person before? If not, consider doing so as a purely generous act, without expecting anything in return.

2. Now imagine that this person approaches you with a problem or a struggle they are facing. This might be something that they are truly going through that they have shared with you, or you might use your imagination for the sake of the practice. Write down how you would respond to this person, being the best possible friend to them that you can be. What body language might you use? What would your tone of voice sound like? What might you say?
   - Next, think about a challenge or struggle that *you* are experiencing right now. How are you responding to your own difficult situation right now? What does your own inner dialogue sound like? What tone of voice does your inner dialogue have? What sort of body language do you have when thinking about your own struggles?
   - Reflect: What are the key differences between how I respond to my loved one and how I respond to myself?

3. Now send yourself a warm blessing. Feel free to come up with your own, or you may use or modify this one:

   *May I be safe. May I be protected from harm and feel a sense of ease. May I find strength and wisdom in the challenges that life has thrown at me. May I feel supported and unafraid. May I always care for myself as I would care for a loved one.*

- Just notice whatever sensations arise in your body, and whatever thoughts or emotions come to mind. What comes up for you? Perhaps you experience a sense of rejection or disgust in your body. Perhaps you feel lighter, warmer. If needed, consider modifying the blessing and trying different versions on for size, until you find one that feels settling in your body. For additional support, consider placing a hand over your heart so you feel your heartbeat, taking a few deep breaths, or going for a short walk.

- When you are ready, revisit the challenging situation you are experiencing and try to respond to yourself with the same compassion and respect that you sent to your loved one. Write down what you might say to yourself, cultivating that loving-kindness toward yourself. Observe any shifts in your bodily sensations, thoughts, and emotions.

4. Bring to mind a person whom you find it very difficult to love, with whom you have a strained relationship, or whom you feel misunderstood by. This should probably be someone that is in your life and for whom the strained relationship causes some distress in a family, social, or workplace dynamic, and with whom you would like to reconcile but may not know how. Write down their name.

   - Take some deep breaths as you bring an image of this person to your mind. Notice what feelings or physical sensations come up for you as you visualize this person. If you begin to experience tension, feel your heart rate start to pick up, or notice any changes in your breathing, simply note these, and continue to breathe.
   - As you settle into your breath, imagine this person. Think about their humanity, struggles they may have been through, and the life experiences that may have made them into the person they are today. Imagine a brick wall between you and this person, and as you breathe, imagine the wall dissolving, brick by brick.
   - When you are ready, begin to send this person a genuine blessing. You may certainly come up with your own, or you may use or modify the following:

     *May you be safe. May you be protected from harm and feel a sense of ease. May you find strength and wisdom in the challenges that life has thrown at you. May we begin to see the humanity in one another.*

5. Finally, spend a few moments meditating on the notion that we cannot change others, only ourselves, and only if we have the desire, motivation, and commitment to change.

6. At the culmination of this practice, bring your awareness back into the present moment. Reflect on this experience of what it felt like to send loving-kindness toward a loved one, toward yourself, and toward someone you have conflict with. Which part was the hardest for you? What interesting sensations did you observe in your body? What, if anything, might you bring forward from this type of visualization in your daily life?

## CHAPTER 6

# Harness Your Strengths

Tapping into our greatest areas of strengths—while still honoring and processing, and without trivializing our suffering—can be incredibly useful for fostering healing and even triumphing in the wake of great adversity and trauma. However, far too many of us are detached from a mindful awareness of what our greatest strengths are in the first place. Today, if someone asked you, "What are your greatest strengths?" what might you say? Take a moment to reflect on how you'd answer that question, without reading ahead to the rest of the chapter.

Practice withholding judgment of yourself, no matter what arises as you think about your response. Many people find this question to be quite difficult to answer[1] or simply haven't given it much thought.

## MY GREATEST STRENGTHS

Now, looking at your answer, how many of your responses mentioned the following:

- Talents (things you excel at, *e.g.,* playing an instrument, sports, cooking)
- Interests (what you enjoy, *e.g.,* activism, music, politics, psychology, medicine)
- Skills (proficiencies you have, *e.g.,* speaking multiple languages, a black belt)
- Resources (external supports that you have access to, *e.g.,* having a great job, making a good salary)

Maybe you left the section completely blank, unable to access anything that you consider to be a strength.

Did anything you jotted down represent strengths of *character*?

While each of these other types of positive qualities (talents, interests, skills, resources) may be important sources of fulfillment in our lives, our *character strengths* in particular may be potent catalysts for coping and overcoming life stress. As Ryan Niemiec, education director of the VIA Institute on Character, a global nonprofit organization devoted to educating people on the science and practice of character strengths, has written: "Talents can be squandered, skills can diminish, and resources lost, but strengths crystalize and evolve and can integrate with these other positive qualities to contribute to the greater good."[2] Let's dive into a brief history on character strengths and the common language of strengths to build awareness of, develop, and apply these character strengths mindfully in our lives.

## A BRIEF HISTORY OF CHARACTER STRENGTHS AND VIRTUES

One of the most significant projects that ensued in the early years of positive psychology at the turn of the twenty-first century was a three-year collaboration among fifty-five psychologists and researchers, led by the late Dr. Christopher Peterson, to uncover a common language of character strengths and virtues that would be valid across ages, genders, and distinct cultures around the globe—including fifty-two nations, from Kenya, to northern Greenland, to the Western world.[3] Today, *Character Strengths & Virtues: A Handbook and Classification*,[4] authored by Martin Seligman and Christopher Peterson, serves as a positive counterpart to the *Diagnostic and Statistical Manual* (*DSM*), the bible of psychiatric diagnoses, by cataloging twenty-four universal character strengths that fall into six categories of virtue (see the table below).

| VIA CLASSIFICATION OF CHARACTER STRENGTHS AND VIRTUES[5] |
|---|
| **1. WISDOM AND KNOWLEDGE:** COGNITIVE STRENGTHS THAT HELP INDIVIDUALS GATHER AND USE KNOWLEDGE. |
| • **Creativity** [originality, ingenuity]: Thinking of new ways to do and conceptualize things. Includes originality (the generation of novel or unusual ideas or behaviors) and adaptiveness (ideas are useful and make a positive contribution to one's life).<br>• **Curiosity** [interest, novelty-seeking, openness to experience]: Taking an interest in ongoing experience for its own sake; a natural desire to build knowledge, finding answers, engaging in new experiences, learning something new.<br>• **Judgment** [critical thinking, open-mindedness]: Thinking things through and examining them from all sides; not jumping to conclusions; being open and able to change one's mind, consider evidence, and weigh all evidence fairly.<br>• **Love of learning:** Mastering new skills, topics, and bodies of knowledge, formally or on one's own initiative; related to curiosity, but goes beyond it to describe the tendency to add systematically to one's knowledge base.<br>• **Perspective** [wisdom]: The ability to provide wise counsel to others; looking at the world in a way that makes sense to one's self and others. |
| **2. COURAGE:** EMOTIONAL STRENGTHS THAT INVOLVE THE EXERCISE OF WILL TO ACCOMPLISH GOALS IN THE FACE OF ADVERSITY OR OPPOSITION (INTERNAL OR EXTERNAL). |
| • **Bravery** [valor]: Facing threat, challenge, difficulty, or pain head-on; speaking up for what's right, even if there's opposition; acting on convictions, even if unpopular; includes but not limited to physical bravery.<br>• **Honesty** [authenticity, integrity]: Speaking truth, presenting oneself in a genuine way, and acting sincerely; taking responsibility for one's feelings and actions; being without pretense.<br>• **Perseverance** [persistence, industriousness]: Finishing what one starts; working through a course of action despite obstacles; taking pleasure in completing tasks; "getting it done."<br>• **Zest** [vitality, enthusiasm, vigor, energy]: Approaching life with excitement and energy; doing things fully and wholeheartedly; living life as an adventure. |

## VIA CLASSIFICATION OF CHARACTER STRENGTHS AND VIRTUES

### 3. HUMANITY: INTERPERSONAL STRENGTHS THAT INVOLVE TENDING TO AND EMBRACING OTHERS.

- **Kindness** [generosity, nurturance, care, compassion, altruism]: Doing favors and good deeds for others; helping people; caring for them.
- **Love** [ability to love, be loved, accept love]: Valuing close relationships with others, in particular, those in which sharing and caring are reciprocated; being close to people.
- **Social intelligence** [emotional intelligence, personal intelligence]: Being aware of the motives/ feelings of others and oneself; knowing what to do to fit into different social situations; knowing what makes other people tick.

### 4. JUSTICE: CIVIC STRENGTHS THAT UNDERLIE HEALTHY COMMUNITY LIFE.

- **Fairness:** Treating all people according to notions of fairness and justice; not letting feelings bias decisions about others; giving everyone a fair chance.
- **Leadership:** Encouraging a group of which one is a member to get things done and maintain high-quality relationships among members; organizing group activities and seeing that they happen.
- **Teamwork** [citizenship, social responsibility, loyalty]: Working well as a member of a group or team; being a "team player"; pulling one's weight.

### 5. TEMPERANCE: STRENGTHS THAT PROTECT AGAINST EXCESS.

- **Forgiveness** [mercy]: Forgiving those who have transgressed; accepting others' shortcomings; giving people a second chance; not being vengeful.
- **Humility** [modesty]: Letting one's accomplishments speak for themselves; not regarding oneself as more special than one is.
- **Prudence:** Taking care in making choices; avoiding undue risks; refraining from saying or doing things that one might regret.
- **Self-regulation** [self-control]: Regulating what one feels and does; being disciplined; controlling one's appetites and emotions.

### 6. TRANSCENDENCE: STRENGTHS THAT FORGE CONNECTIONS WITH THE UNIVERSE AND PROVIDE MEANING.

- **Appreciation of beauty and excellence** [awe, wonder, elevation]: Noticing and appreciating beauty, excellence, and/or skilled performance in various domains of life, including nature, art, mathematics, science, and everyday experience.
- **Gratitude:** Being aware of and thankful for the good things that happen, taking time to express thanks.
- **Hope** [optimism, future-mindedness, future orientation]: Expecting the best in the future and working to achieve it; believing that a good future is something that can be brought about.
- **Humor** [playfulness]: Liking to laugh and tease; bringing smiles to other people; seeing the light side; making (not necessarily telling) jokes.

| VIA CLASSIFICATION OF CHARACTER STRENGTHS AND VIRTUES |
| --- |
| **6. TRANSCENDENCE: STRENGTHS THAT FORGE CONNECTIONS WITH THE UNIVERSE AND PROVIDE MEANING.** |
| · **Spirituality** [religiousness, faith, purpose]: Having coherent beliefs about the higher purpose and meaning of the universe; knowing where one fits within the larger scheme; having beliefs about the meaning of life that shape conduct and provide comfort. |

*Reproduced with permission from the VIA institute*

These twenty-four character strengths are positive personality traits that contribute to both personal fulfillment and good for the world.[6] Everyone has their own distinct profile and unique combination of strengths that reflect both who we are and what we do. Each strength serves a different function in our lives, and there is no hierarchy among them.

Additionally, strengths are not fixed traits across settings and time, but rather they are malleable, subject to growth, and context-specific.[7] We have higher strengths, known as "signature strengths," which are those that are the most aligned with our authentic self and transcend context; these are the core facets of our identity.

While there is no set number of signature strengths that an individual has, conventional wisdom suggests that we have anywhere from three to seven, though some report as many as nine.[8] Our signature strengths are intrinsically motivated, help us feel energized, and may be called upon to help us overcome challenges and trauma. They can also help boost our lesser strengths, which are those strengths that may come less naturally but are nonetheless present and can be cultivated. Our lesser strengths are not necessarily weaknesses.

Niemiec states that there is a pervasive lack of deep mindfulness in our society when it comes to our strengths. He states four specific ways that we may be blind to strengths:[9]

1. **General unawareness of strengths:** As you may have experienced firsthand at the opening of this chapter when asked to reflect on your own strengths, many people find this simple act incredibly challenging. We are generally not cultured or encouraged to think about our best qualities! We hope that this is rapidly changing as the work of organizations like the VIA Institute and Character Lab[10] permeate school

curricula and cultures around the globe. For now, we must take this opportunity to learn the language of strengths (starting with the table from the previous pages) to enhance our awareness and begin thinking about ourselves and others in these terms.

2. **Disconnection between strengths and their meaning:** According to one survey, about two-thirds of people have no meaningful awareness of their character strengths and how these serve them in daily life.[11] Even for those who can answer the question "What are your best qualities?" these answers are frequently vague or refer to talents, skills, interests, or resources. Most of us do not make meaningful connections as to how our character underlies our own achievements, goals, ability to overcome challenges, or values in life.

3. **Seeing strengths as ordinary, rather than extraordinary:** When people do identify or talk about their character strengths, we tend to quickly gloss over them, thinking that these are just normal phenomena that can be taken for granted; *"Of course I love the people in my life . . . this isn't anything special . . ."* However, research reveals that there is almost always something more that can be drawn from our strengths, including new ways that strengths can be used in challenging situations, or how to tap into a top strength to reach a particular goal. Certainly, we can all benefit from using more of our strengths in our work, at home, and in coping with the stress of human life.

4. **Overusing our strengths:** It's important to consider that strengths can have maladaptive consequences when they are used in excess or in inappropriate settings. Character strengths are not just blunt instruments that we should throw indiscriminately into all settings; rather, there is a "golden mean," or right combination of strengths, degree of use, and situation that will optimally benefit both ourselves and others.[12] (See the table on the next page, which outlines ideas around the underuse, overuse, and optimal use of each strength.)[13] For example, as a physician, if Jordyn used her strength of humor when telling a patient about a terminal diagnosis, this would likely be perceived as insensitive and wildly inappropriate. When it comes to strengths, there can certainly be too much of a good thing.

| CHARACTER STRENGTH | UNDERUSE | OVERUSE | OPTIMAL USE |
|---|---|---|---|
| **Appreciation of Beauty and Excellence** | Mindless, oblivious, stuck in autopilot, unaware of beauty | Snobbish, perfectionistic | Awe- and wonderstruck, admires excellence, elevates the goodness of others |
| **Bravery** | Cowardly, unwilling to be vulnerable, unwilling to act or stand up for oneself or one's beliefs | Risk-taking, foolhardy, overconfident, brazen | Fear-facing, unafraid of adversity, valorous, stands up for beliefs |
| **Creativity** | Conforming, unimaginative, trite | Scattered, bizarre, erratic | Unique, clever, imaginative |
| **Curiosity** | Uninterested, bored, apathetic, self-involved | Intrusive, nosy, meddlesome | Exploratory, intrigued, open, novelty-seeking |
| **Fairness** | Prejudiced, immoral, complacent, unjust | Detached, overly impartial, indecisive | Champion of equal opportunity for all, justice-oriented, strong moral compass |
| **Forgiveness** | Vengeful, merciless, bitter, resentful, grudge-holder | Permissive, spineless, doormat | Able to let go and move on when wronged, giver of second chances, self-respecting |
| **Gratitude** | Entitled, unappreciative, rude, self-absorbed | Ingratiating, contrived, profuse | Thankful, connected, appreciative, seeks the good |
| **Honesty** | Phony, inauthentic, lacking integrity, deceitful | Self-righteous, inconsiderate, oversharing | Authentic, truth-seeking, truth-sharing, sincere, without pretense |
| **Hope** | Despairing, pessimistic, living in the past, cynical | Unrealistic, blindly optimistic, head-in-the clouds, "rose-colored glasses" | Optimistic, confident in the future, expects positive things to happen |
| **Humility** | Arrogant, braggadocio, narcissistic | Self-deprecating, subservient, self-conscious | Clear view of oneself, modest, aware of one's own limitations, focused on others |

| CHARACTER STRENGTH | UNDERUSE | OVERUSE | OPTIMAL USE |
|---|---|---|---|
| **Humor** | Flat, humorless, overly serious, stifled, stiff | Tasteless, offensive, out of touch | Joy/laughter-seeking, sees the lighter side of life, playful |
| **Judgment** | Illogical, naïve, closed-minded, gullible | Rigid, narrow-minded, indecisive, lost in one's head | Analytical, detail-oriented, open-minded, rational, logical |
| **Kindness** | Mean-spirited, cruel, indifferent, selfish, uncaring | Compassion-fatigued, overly focused on others | Doing for others and oneself, caring, compassionate to others and self, friendly |
| **Leadership** | Passive, thoughtlessly compliant, follower | Bossy, controlling, authoritarian, "my way or the highway" | Positively influences others, organizes people, leads around a vision |
| **Love** | Detached, isolated, cut off, empty, lonely, cold | Emotional overkill, saccharine, disingenuous warmth | Warm, connected, relationally fulfilled, generous of spirit |
| **Love of Learning** | Smug, uninterested, complacent with current knowledge | Know-it-all, elitist | Information-seeking, lifelong learner |
| **Perseverance** | Lazy, helpless, unmotivated | Stubborn, fixated, unable to let go | Task completer, gritty, persistent, hardworking |
| **Perspective** | Superficial, shallow, foolish | Disconnected, overbearing, arrogant | Wise, perceptive, sensible, able to integrate multiple viewpoints |
| **Prudence** | Reckless, ill-advised, negligent, thoughtless | Stuffy, prudish, rigid, cagey | Wisely cautious, planner, goal-oriented, manages risk |
| **Self-regulation** | Self-indulgent, impulsive, lacking discipline, unfocused | Inhibited, tightly wound, obsessive | Self-manager of vices, disciplined, mindful, focused |

| CHARACTER STRENGTH | UNDERUSE | OVERUSE | OPTIMAL USE |
|---|---|---|---|
| **Social Intelligence** | Clueless, unaware, disconnected, obtuse, insensitive | Overanalytical, overly sensitive, psychobabbling | Tuned in, savvy, knows what makes others tick, empathic, emotionally intelligent |
| **Spirituality** | Nihilistic, disconnected from purpose, meaning, and values | Proselytizing, preachy, fanatical, holier-than-thou | Connected to the sacred, pursues meaningfulness, expresses virtue |
| **Teamwork** | Individualistic, self-serving | Prone to groupthink, blind obedience, dependent, lacking sense of self | Participative, loyal, socially responsible, collaborative |
| **Zest** | Sedentary, tired, lifeless | Hyperactive, annoying | Vital, enthusiastic, active, energized |

*Chart courtesy VIA Institute*

Niemiec discusses the critical integration of character strengths with mindfulness to deliberately work through each of these forms of strengths blindness and optimally bring forth our strengths in our lives. In his seminal book, *Mindfulness & Character Strengths: A Practical Guide to Flourishing*, he writes:

> *"Put simply, mindfulness opens a door of awareness to who we are, and character strengths are what is behind the door since character strengths are who we at our core. Mindfulness opens the door to potential self-improvement and growth while character use is often the growth itself."*

In pursuit of this integration, Niemiec has successfully developed an 8-week strengths-based mindfulness program called Mindfulness-Based Strengths Practice (MBSP) that is used across the globe in more than fifty countries.[14] Here, we present a path forward for beginning to mindfully identify and attend to our own character strengths and those of others, experiment with using our strengths in new ways, and spot strengths in ourselves and others.

# KNOW YOUR STRENGTHS

## PRACTICE

1. The first step of this practice is to spend some time really studying the language of strengths presented in the VIA Classification of Character Strengths and Virtues table. Actively read and reread this table, which includes the six virtues and twenty-four strengths with their synonyms and definitions. Start to use these words in daily life, write them down, converse with others in this language. The more agile we are with the language of strengths, the more these will come to life for us as we start to see them in real time in ourselves and others.

    • As you read through this table, are there any of these strengths that stand out to you that you think might be among your signature strengths? One way to get at whether a strength is a signature strength is to ask yourself, "If I couldn't use this strength in my life, would I be me?"

2. A fantastic way to attain a valid measure of your twenty-four strengths is by taking the VIA survey. Do so by visiting www.viacharacter.org and click "take the free survey." Register on the VIA Institute on Character website and create your account. Choose the adult version of the survey and answer all the questions until you reach your results.

    Note: Your top five results will automatically appear. You can click "show all of your strengths" to view the entire twenty-four.

    • Reflect: Are you tempted to scroll all the way to the bottom to view your lesser strengths before reading through your top strengths? If so, you are not alone! Remember, we are wired to overattend to potential threats or the negative features in our environments! Remember, lesser strengths are not weaknesses. Can you bring mindful awareness to and withhold judgment for all your strengths, including those that are lowest on your list?

3. Once you reveal your list according to the VIA survey, examine the top ten. Ask yourself the following questions:

- How do the strengths that I identified as possible signature strengths fall within my list? Do these appear in my top ten?
- Do these top strengths come naturally to me?
- Have others in my life, including family and friends, observed these strengths in me?
- How do I express these strengths across different settings?

At this point, you have likely nailed down three to ten of your signature strengths.

# EXPLORE YOUR STRENGTHS

## PRACTICE

Once you feel aware of and agile with the language of character strengths and have identified how the twenty-four are ranked for you at this moment, spend some time pondering one of your signature strengths. You can do this for each strength if that is helpful, but we recommend starting from the top.[15]

- What does it look like for me to express this strength? What does it feel like in my body to express this strength?
- When and where do I use this strength regularly in my daily life?
- How do I use this strength when I am feeling my best?
- How do I use this strength in times of stress?
- In what situations might I overexpress this strength?
- In what situations might I underexpress this strength?
- What benefits does this strength bring me and others in my life?

Rinse and repeat with other strengths on your list!

The next step is to begin mindfully integrating strengths into our daily lives. We can do this two primary ways:

1. Spotting strengths (in others and ourselves).

2. Using strengths in new ways.

# SPOT STRENGTHS IN OTHERS

## PRACTICE

- Once we feel that we are well versed in the language of strengths and have thought deeply about some of our own top strengths, we can begin *noticing* these strengths in real time in both ourselves and others. When we notice the use of strengths, we may label them, call them out, and highlight the specific behaviors that reveal the strength.
- When spotting strengths in others—for instance, a friend who gives you sound advice on how to deal with a difficult work situation—we may notice them using the strength of perspective and say: "Wow, you have such a fantastic way of seeing all sides of a situation. You are so wise; perspective is totally one of your signature strengths."

Strengths-spotting in this way has a multitude of benefits. First, talking about strengths we notice with others is a way to savor the positive effects of using strengths (see the "Savor Life" practice in chapter 8). It is also a way to strengthen the quality of our connections and possibly reinforce our partner's ideal selves (see "The Statue of David and You" in chapter 5). It may also inspire curiosity in others to learn more about what you mean when you mention "signature strengths," if they are not familiar with the concept (this can be one way to foster intellectual curiosity; see "Open Your Mind" in chapter 4). This provides an opportunity to introduce others to your newly acquired language of strengths; you can always send them a link to the VIA survey and talk about your results together. This will not only expand the reach of this critically important concept, but it will also expand the network of individuals who can speak the language with you!

# USE STRENGTHS IN NEW WAYS

## PRACTICE

In replicated, randomized, online placebo-controlled trials, research participants who were asked to identify and use a top personal strength in a new way every day for only one week were found to have increased happiness and decreased depression up to six months later.[16]

- How can you mindfully deploy one of your top strengths in a novel way each day this week?

The VIA Institute on Character website has fantastic recommendations for new ways to use each character strength that you can access after taking your VIA survey. We have included a brief set of recommendations in the table on the following pages. Set yourself up to deliberately use your strengths this week.

- Want to take it to the next level? Think about how you might use a top strength to help enhance a lesser strength.
- When a challenging situation arises in real time, use a top strength to address it. In any given situation, it will be important to think about:[17]
  - *Relevance:* Does the situation require a strength?
  - *Conflict:* What strength should I use, especially if multiple strengths are competing?
  - *Specificity:* What is needed to translate the strength into action?

And now let's revisit the question that started us off at the top of this chapter. What are your greatest strengths? And why?

## MY GREATEST STRENGTHS

<br>

| USING STRENGTHS IN NEW WAYS[18] | |
|---|---|
| **Appreciation of Beauty and Excellence** | · Spend twenty minutes standing still outside in a beautiful natural environment.<br>· Visit an art gallery, attend a concert, or simply listen to a piece of music that is viewed to be extraordinary; let yourself be overtaken by what you experience. Ponder the talent that went into producing such work.<br>· Keep a beauty log: Write a few sentences about something beautiful you see or experience. |
| **Bravery** | · Reach out to and befriend someone who is new and different from you.<br>· Take on a new adventure or hobby you have been wanting to try.<br>· Identify an area that you might shy away from. Practice ways to effectively confront the situation. |
| **Creativity** | · Write a poem or creative writing piece, or try making art or music.<br>· Cook a new dish by using only ingredients you currently have in your home.<br>· When facing a problem, define the issue and brainstorm multiple possible solutions or outcomes.<br>· Turn an ordinary household object, such as a paper clip or toothpick, into something meaningful. |
| **Curiosity** | · Explore your environment, paying attention to details you might not ordinarily notice.<br>· Pick a new podcast to listen to about a topic you know little about.<br>· Try a new food from another culture for the first time.<br>· Try a different route on a daily commute than you normally take, and explore a new neighborhood or setting. |

| USING STRENGTHS IN NEW WAYS | |
| --- | --- |
| **Fairness** | • Include someone in a conversation who may be a newcomer, or who may be excluded from a group that you are a part of.<br>• Apologize to someone who you may have wronged or made a mistake with.<br>• Pay attention to how you treat people around you who have different levels of power or positions. Make a conscious effort to treat everyone right. |
| **Forgiveness** | • Write about a negative incident or grudge you held, and consider any doors that opened for you or benefits you experienced after the incident.<br>• Think about someone who wronged you recently and try to look at the situation from their side.<br>• Vow to forgive yourself for a mistake you made recently. |
| **Gratitude** | • Write down three good things that you are grateful for each day, and why you're grateful for them.<br>• Go out of your way to tell someone who deserves it, but may not be recognized, "Thanks."<br>• Send a note of gratitude to someone via email, text, or a Post-it note on their desk or at their workplace.<br>• Keep a gratitude journal: Write in it whenever you are struck with a sensation of gratitude. |
| **Honesty** | • Write a poem or create a piece of art that expresses an inner truth.<br>• Honor commitments in all your relationships. Don't flake on plans you've made with others.<br>• Check in with yourself—are your actions consistent with your intentions and values? Make necessary changes where needed.<br>• Contact someone who you might have told a partial truth to and let them know the full story. |
| **Hope** | • Think about a problem you are experiencing and come up with one or two realistic, optimistic thoughts about how the problem might be addressed.<br>• Reflect or write about a time when you took action to enhance a situation for yourself or for another person.<br>• Set positive goals for yourself and picture yourself overcoming obstacles. |
| **Humility** | • Resist showing off accomplishments for a week and notice changes in your relationships.<br>• During conversations, pay attention to how much you speak relative to others; if you are doing more of the talking/sharing, practice flipping it to allow the other person to talk/share more.<br>• Admit your mistakes and apologize when you are in the wrong.<br>• Ask someone you trust for feedback on potential areas for growth. |

| USING STRENGTHS IN NEW WAYS | |
|---|---|
| **Humor** | · Keep a humor log: Write down a funny thing that happens each day (even things that are not necessarily laugh-out-loud funny, but that are amusing).<br>· Watch a comedy or sitcom, read a comic or a funny blog—allow yourself to laugh out loud.<br>· Do something spontaneous and playful when you are with another person. |
| **Judgment** | · Watch a political program from a network that has an opposite point of view from your own and keep an open mind!<br>· Play devil's advocate on an issue you have a strong opinion about (kindly, asking clarifying questions).<br>· Evaluate a past event that you are unhappy with and brainstorm alternative solutions. |
| **Kindness** | · Offer to drop off a healthy meal to an elderly neighbor's home.<br>· Perform a random act of kindness every day this week (*e.g.*, volunteering, sending kind words to a loved one, calling an isolated or elderly member of the family).<br>· Speak kinder and softer words to people in emails and conversations. |
| **Leadership** | · Take the lead on an activity or project and actively ask for opinions for group members; delegate tasks based on the strengths of your group members.<br>· Mediate an argument between people in conflict; encourage them to share openly and find solutions.<br>· Discuss with someone who reports to you how they can align their top character strength more in their work. |
| **Love** | · Write a note to or plan a surprise for someone you love or appreciate.<br>· Engage in a meaningful activity with a loved one (including someone you might be physically with or distanced from).<br>· Tell someone about a strength you saw them use and how much you value it. |
| **Love of Learning** | · Learn five new words a day.<br>· Host or attend an in-person or virtual interest group/salon/book club.<br>· Download a language-learning application and begin practicing a new language.<br>· Follow some of the citations throughout this book and discover new books to read; read the original research papers!<br>· Take a master class, an online course, or a live course on a topic you wish to learn more about. |
| **Perseverance** | · Set one or two realistic goals per day, and think about the obstacles that may come up; think about how you will face the obstacles to accomplish your goal(s).<br>· Complete a small project that you have been putting off. |

| USING STRENGTHS IN NEW WAYS | |
| --- | --- |
| **Perspective** | · Deliberately focus and listen carefully to others before sharing your thoughts.<br>· Read an article by someone with a different opinion using an open mind.<br>· Consider some of the wisest people you know. Think about how they might handle a difficult situation that you find yourself in. |
| **Prudence** | · Before making a quick decision that might seem like a no-brainer, take a minute or so to think through your options.<br>· Write about the costs and benefits of taking a particular action as well as the costs and benefits of not taking a particular action. Review the results to consider the most practical decision. |
| **Self-regulation** | · Practice deliberate breathing and paying attention to the sensations in your body before reflexively acting during a stressful situation.<br>· Set daily goals for disciplined living (*e.g.,* cleaning, doing laundry, eating well, getting physical exercise). Monitor and document what you do through a checklist or tracking sheet. |
| **Social Intelligence** | · Initiate a conversation with a stranger, such as a waiter, someone on the street, a fellow restaurant patron, or a cabdriver.<br>· Practice expressing your emotions to those around you directly, labeling your feelings and explaining how the emotion feels for you.<br>· Practice noticing emotions in others and inquiring about these in a nonjudgmental way: *"I notice you looked a bit disappointed after our last meeting, do you want to talk about it?"* or *"You seem so excited about your vacation next week, what are you most excited about?"* |
| **Spirituality** | · Cultivate moments in your day to "just be" with a special object or place, and meditate on the significance of the moment.<br>· Build time for prayer, meditation, or time in nature into your daily routine.<br>· Develop a new ritual with a loved one. |
| **Teamwork** | · Volunteer your time to an organization, or consider mentoring a junior colleague, a friend, or a family member.<br>· Spot and express appreciation for the strengths demonstrated by your team members. Invite them to take the VIA survey and share your results!<br>· Savor a positive team interaction by debriefing it in a team meeting. |
| **Zest** | · Engage in physical activities (biking, running, yoga, singing, play) and take active breaks in your day.<br>· Express your energy through an outfit, a pair of shoes, and/or accessories that represent who you are.<br>· Share positive news with people in your life to boost enthusiasm and energy; help others capitalize on the positive news that they share with you by asking questions to help them relive positive experiences. |

*Table courtesy VIA Institute*

## CHAPTER 7

# Live Your Purpose

Happiness is an epiphenomenon, a by-product,
something not to be sought directly but an indirect reward for virtue . . .
The only happy people I know are the ones who are working well
at something they consider important.[1]
—Abraham Maslow, 1962

If one does not know to which port one is sailing,
no wind is favorable.
—Seneca

Everything can be taken from a man but one thing:
the last of human freedoms—to choose one's attitude in any
given set of circumstances, to choose one's own way.
—Viktor Frankl, 1946

There is a great paradox to the pursuit of happiness: When we chase it head-on, it only seems to get farther and farther away. Psychologists refer to this as the "hedonic treadmill"; chasing pleasures, unbalanced by a sense of purpose and engagement in the world, can leave us staggering in place, asking ourselves, *"Is this really what life is all about?"*

A full life is driven by our uniquely human desire to leave our mark on the world, a phenomenon that philosopher and novelist Rebecca Goldstein calls the "mattering instinct."[2] There are many different paths to mattering, but one potentially strong route is through having and living with purpose. Our need for purpose can be defined as the need for an overarching aspiration that energizes our efforts and provides a central source of meaning and significance in our lives. Having such a purpose can cause a fundamental reordering of our most central motives. With a purpose, things that once preoccupied us can suddenly feel trivial.[3]

For many of us, especially youth today, it can be so tempting to view images of grandeur and celebrity on social media and see fame as a compelling, unifying conduit for living our purpose. However, author Emily Esfahani Smith points to a growing body of research confirming that meaning and purpose are not found through success or glamour, but rather in things that are mundane: chipping in to help our families when a loved one is sick, volunteering our time to those in need within our communities, or simply helping to cheer up a friend.[4] If we are really lucky, our jobs and livelihoods may be avenues for living purposefully as well.

Organizational psychologist Amy Wrzesniewski and her colleagues have found that people who view their everyday jobs as a calling, a central force in one's life that they would do even if they didn't get paid, report greater levels of life satisfaction and job satisfaction and miss fewer days at work compared to those who view their work as simply a job or career.[5] These findings hold even when researchers control for income, education, and occupation, suggesting that satisfaction with life and with work may depend more on our relationship to the work than the income it yields or how prestigious the work is.

How often when we meet someone, do we ask them, "What do you do?" And just how seldom do we follow up with, "Why do you do it?" It is this second, often unasked, question that gets to our purpose. As Maslow put it, "What's not worth doing is not worth doing well."[6]

Now, what do these findings mean in this moment, when we have just experienced a "great resignation" in America and, for some, simply having the stability of any job is supposed to feel like a luxury? What about for those of us who have really struggled to adapt to changing work environments, and may have lost touch with the most meaningful and engaging parts of our work? What about the vast majority of people on the planet who find their jobs monotonous, lacking in importance, or even soul-crushing, and would quit tomorrow if they had the financial stability to do so?

For one, each of us can try to find and connect with the threads of purpose in what we do and tend to those aspects—even the minor ones—that link our daily tasks and routines to something larger—our *why*. For example, an advertising rep for a travel company might spend a few minutes every day thinking about how her daily tasks selling ad space might contribute to another person's ability to see the world and experience new cultures and places on the planet; a food service worker who delivers meals might consider how his work brings people together over hot food and helps a family-owned restaurant transform into a takeout operation. Our relationship to the work we do matters, and we can deliberately *seek* the purpose and connect with it regularly.[7]

We can also craft meaning in our jobs by reengineering and reconceptualizing tasks and relationships at work to be more aligned with our strengths, values, and passions, an intervention known as "job crafting."[8] Perhaps the travel rep expands her role to create new partnerships with advertisers from companies oriented toward sustainability or those invested in creating jobs in underserved communities; the food service worker might partner with a fellow employee to bring food leftovers to a local shelter or a family in need.

We might also move on from our current situations and seek new opportunities that are more closely aligned with our values. And at the same time, while work may be a powerful well and opportunity for purpose, it need not be our sole source—we can tap into meaning outside of work through hobbies and volunteering, and through our networks of family and friends. The practices in this chapter are designed to help us all reflect on our sources of meaning and purpose and how we might recenter these in our lives.

## WHAT DO YOU VALUE?

Have you ever been asked to reflect on your greatest, most deeply held values in life? If so, what has come to mind? If not, you are most definitely not alone. When we have asked hundreds of our students over the last several years to explicitly contemplate what they value most in life, we are always amazed by how few people have done this before. It is astonishing because our values are a critical component of ourselves and, whether we are consciously aware of it or not, guide our behaviors in profound ways.[9]

According to cross-cultural values researcher Shalom H. Schwartz, *values* refers to desirable goals that motivate action and serve as guiding principles in the life of a person or group.[10] Our values are infused with strong feelings, especially when they are activated or violated in some way (think about a person who strongly values independence and individual freedom who becomes infuriated by mask mandates; or the person who strongly values public health who is furious with those who refuse to take vaccines).

Accordingly, our values may conflict with others' values, or even other values that we hold ourselves, which may lead to both interpersonal and intrapersonal conflict. Certainly, we are all seeing such conflicts play out in our own communities and on the national and global stages. Our values may guide how we choose certain actions, policies, political leaders, and communities, and tend to transcend context, guiding our global motivations and behaviors.

Schwartz's *The Refined Theory of Basic Human Values* outlines nineteen motivationally distinct values and the dynamic relations among them that are recognized across all major cultures.[11] See the circle figure from Jan Cieciuch and colleagues on the next page.

Inherent in this model are the dynamic relations among the values, including how pursuing actions in line with one value has consequences that may be congruent or in conflict with other values. As shown in the figure, values displayed opposite one another, such as openness to change and conservation, and self-enhancement and self-transcendence values, may conflict (although, as we discuss throughout this book, we can certainly pursue goals that integrate both higher-order values, such as "healthy selfishness"; see chapter 3). Another interesting facet of this model is the distinction between universalism, or love for the world, and benevolence, or love for the in-group, a distinction we also try to make throughout this book.

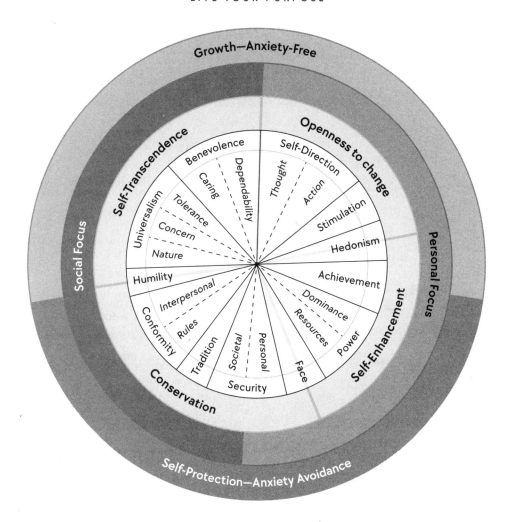

We present this model to highlight how certain values may be more closely aligned with one another and other values may have more inherent conflict. Here is an even more comprehensive list of values:

| | | | |
|---|---|---|---|
| Acceptance | Arts | Calm | Communication |
| Activism | Attentiveness | Caring | Community |
| Adventure | Balance | Citizenship | Compassion |
| Altruism | Belonging | Charity | Connectedness |

| | | | |
|---|---|---|---|
| Courage | Health | Openness | Simplicity |
| Creativity | History | Order | Spirituality |
| Curiosity | Honor | Organization | Spontaneity |
| Discipline | Human rights | Patience | Stability |
| Diversity | Humor | Peace | Stewardship |
| Education | Imagination | Perseverance | Strength |
| Effort | Independence | Philanthropy | Structure |
| Environmentalism | Integrity | Play | Sustainability |
| Equity | Intelligence | Positivity | Thoughtfulness |
| Excitement | Intimacy | Power | Tolerance |
| Expansiveness | Intuition | Productivity | Transcendence |
| Experience | Justice | Reliability | Understanding |
| Faith | Kindness | Respect | Unity |
| Family | Leadership | Rhythm | Warmth |
| Fitness | Learning | Risk | Wisdom |
| Flow | Love | Security | Wit |
| Forgiveness | Loyalty | Self-expression | Wonder |
| Freedom | Magic | Self-sufficiency | |
| Fun | Nesting | Sensuality | |
| Generosity | Nurturance | Serenity | |

For many of us, unpacking our values can help us understand ourselves and our own feelings and behaviors more deeply. This process can also set us on a path to understanding others' feelings and behaviors (including those people or groups that we may disagree or have conflict with). Clarifying our values can also help us make positive changes in our lives that will enable us to live more authentically by our own purpose.

Engaging in these big questions can feel overwhelming, even a bit morally distressing, if we realize there might be a disconnect between the things that matter most to us and the realities of our daily lives.

This practice is about identifying with and subsequently aligning our values with our daily routines, and, in the process, shedding some of our emotional, attentional, and time investments in lesser-valued ideas and activities.

## PRACTICE

1. **Identify your core values.** Spend some time really reflecting on the question "What matters most to me in this world?" You may use the space below as a starting place and reflect on the following questions as a guide; feel free to refer to the list of values provided on pages 131–32 to help spark your thoughts.
   - What guiding principles provide me with a sense of resonance and meaning in my life?
   - What are the values that I'd like to pass on to the next generation?
   - What are the words that I'd want written on my proverbial tombstone to sum up my life if I were to live by my deepest-held values?

MY TOP VALUES

2. **Define your core values.** It's important to note that any two people with ostensibly the same top values may have very different conceptions or definitions of what these values mean to them. Narrow your list down to three to five of your very top core values; how do you define these for yourself? What do your top values mean to you?
   1.
   2.

3.

4.

5.

**How are you living by each of these values daily?** In what capacities are they already showing up in your life? Has this been intentional or more circumstantial?

1.

2.

3.

4.

5.

3. **Reflect:**
- How do some of the values on my list complement or conflict with other values on the list?
- How do these values complement or conflict with the values of other people in my life?
- How do these values complement or conflict with the values of the organizations, workplaces, or other institutions that I am connected to?
- How have my values shifted and transformed over the course of my life?
- How might my values have been operating in my life recently, within the last few years, months, and weeks?

# WHAT'S YOUR *IKIGAI*?

When author, explorer, and founder of Blue Zones Dan Buettner partnered with National Geographic to study the places on Earth where humans live the longest, he and his colleagues distilled some of the cross-cultural underpinnings of a longevity "formula," asking not only how we can add more years to our lives, but also how we can add more "life to our years."[12] Studying cultures from Sardinia, Italy, to Ikaria, Greece, to Okinawa, Japan, Buettner discovered that a purposeful orientation toward life is a common ingredient in these incredibly robust cultures.

One concept found to be central in Okinawa is called *ikigai*, a Japanese concept roughly translating to "reason for being" or "reason to wake up in the morning." Researchers Dean Fido, Yasuhiro Kotera, and Kenichi Asano describe *ikigai* as a "composite construct encompassing meaning, motivation, and values in life."[13] Buettner explains that the notion of "retirement" is absent from the zeitgeist in Okinawa, and rather, well into their hundreds, residents remain actively engaged in the things that bring them great purpose. Whether it's caring for a great-great-grandchild, passing down community traditions to the next generation, teaching karate, or fishing, Okinawans don't just know why they get out of bed in the morning; even at age one hundred, they *actually do it*.

### Ikigai
A Japanese concept meaning "a reason for being"

Satisfaction, but feeling of uselessness

What you love

Delights and fullness, but no wealth

Passion

Mission

What you are good at

*Ikigai*

What the world needs

Profession

Vocation

Comfortable, but feeling of emptiness

What you can be rewarded for

Excitement and complacency, but sense of uncertainty

Albeit difficult to measure and formally study, *ikigai* has been associated with several health benefits, including physical health in the elderly, a reduced incidence of strokes and cardiovascular disease, better mental health, and enhanced psychological well-being of caregivers.[14] According to author Yukari Mitsuhashi, *ikigai* is not just about our overall orientation toward life but is found in the small and seemingly mundane moments of lived experience.

# PRACTICE

Spend some time engaging in quiet reflection on the concept of *ikigai* through the exploration of the following questions.[15]

- How does the concept of *ikigai* resonate for me? What organizing forces in my life are most central in keeping me grounded and connected with a sense of meaning and help me through challenges?
- How have these last few years confirmed or brought into question my reasons for waking up in the morning?

WHAT I'M GOOD AT
- What types of things feel relatively effortless for me? (These can be talents, skills, or strengths of character, which we discussed at length in chapter 6.) What do I excel at even when I am not trying particularly hard?
- What do others call on me to help them with?
- What aspects of my work come most easily to me?

WHAT I LOVE
- What kinds of activities excite me?
- What sorts of things would I do on an "ideal" day?
- If I quit my job tomorrow, what might I do instead (even if I didn't get paid)?
- What do I never get bored of doing?

WHAT THE WORLD NEEDS
- What do I feel is lacking or unjust in the world?
- What types of problems do I most enjoy working on?

- What ideas and people are most inspiring to me?
- What might I do to help my community?

WHAT I CAN BE REWARDED FOR
- Am I fulfilled by the work I'm doing (or the way I'm spending my days)?
- Am I able to support myself and my needs currently (including my family's needs)?
- What type of work do I really want to be doing?
- If money were no object, what would I choose to do?
- What might I do that I'd never want to retire from?

Now convert your reflections above into this blank *ikigai* diagram below:

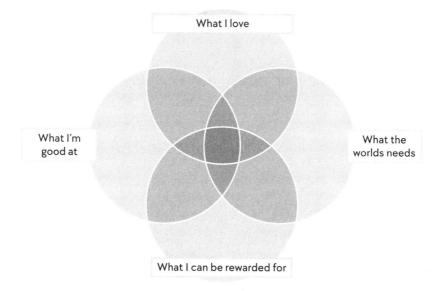

- Reflect on the themes that have emerged from this practice, attending to anything that emerges from the nexus of these questions (narrowing down your *ikigai*). Remember, one's *ikigai* can be dynamic, taking on new dimensions throughout our lives.

- What is one thing I can do to live more in line with my *ikigai*? How might I attend to my *ikigai* on a daily, or at least weekly, basis?

We implore you to engage another person in a conversation about *ikigai*; ask them why they wake up in the morning, and consider teaching them about this idea.

# WHAT'S *YOUR* PANDEMIC STORY?

For decades to come, the era of COVID-19 will provide a common reference point and language for all humans on the planet who lived through this time to connect, share stories, and relate to one another. A conversation starter with a stranger on an airplane, a fellow patron in a restaurant, first-date fodder, tales for our grandchildren one day: We will likely all be talking about this moment in history, and how it changed us, for the rest of our lives.

Stories connect us, reinforce our sense of purpose, and provide us with a path forward to close the gaps between the realities we lead and those which we imagine.[16] They can help us integrate the darkness of our lives into our narrative, and perhaps even emerge from and grow from that darkness. In this practice, we offer you a space to reflect on recent challenges and write about these in an honest, growth-focused way. Consider:

- How might we consider the power that we each have in crafting the meaning that comes from our own experiences?
- How can we take ownership of our own narrative and tell the stories of our lives that only we can tell?
- How might we articulate the impact of this time, and reconcile the sometimes-opposing feelings and experiences of the tragic, mundane, confusing, and beautiful into a cohesive story? Does it even have to be cohesive?
- How might we recognize, uplift, and honor these inherent contradictions of our own stories as a way of more deeply understanding our complex humanity?

As Emily Esfahani Smith notes: "Facing suffering head-on is not an easy task or one that's encouraged in our culture, which values happiness inordinately. Telling or changing our story takes time, and it can be a painful process. But it's a necessary one if we want to move past the brokenness of the COVID-19 era toward a newfound sense of wholeness."[17]

# PRACTICE

Write your pandemic story. Think about what has happened, how the events of this time may have changed you, and what lessons you would like to take with you and share with others from this time. Here are some suggestions and prompts to get your narrative juices flowing. Feel free to use these or disregard them completely; ultimately, this is your story to tell.

- Consider starting with some of the practical details: Where were you when you heard about the quarantine restrictions in your community? How did you feel? Where did you go? What was this initial period like for you? Were there various phases to your pandemic experience?
- Reflect on how the pandemic has changed you. What or whom have you lost? What, if anything, have you gained? What might have come of this time that might not have happened had the pandemic not happened?
- Finally, you might spend time thinking about your story of the future. As you come out of the pandemic, what sort of life do you want to lead? What sort of person do you want to become?

Consider writing your story out—remember, it's your story to tell the way you want to tell it. Perhaps invite others, friends, colleagues, or peers, to write their pandemic stories as well. Share these with one another. If you find this practice to be helpful, consider revisiting the prompts and replacing the pandemic with any traumatic or life-changing event in your life; you are the author of your own narrative.

# WHAT'S YOUR LEGACY?

*Though the physicality of death destroys us,*
*the idea of death may save us.*
—Irvin Yalom[18]

One of the most troubling and potentially traumatic features of pandemic life has been the magnitude of the sudden loss of life for so many humans on the planet. Early on, COVID-infected patients decompensated so rapidly at such a large scale; far too many people lost their lives without the company of loved ones, and without time or warning to fully process or express their wishes or final words. Too many perished not from COVID infection itself, but from related consequences of putting off necessary health-care, or from conditions of despair such as drug overdose or suicide.

For you making your way through this book, you are choosing a path of growth. Part of this growth is honoring and contemplating our own mortality as a means of tapping into our sense of meaning for the precious time that we do have on this Earth. As morbid as it may sound, death awareness and contemplation have been demonstrated in numerous studies to lead to increased helping and sustainability behaviors as well as better health choices, such as using more sunscreen, smoking less, and getting more physical activity.[19] Even in the laboratory, research participants given an opportunity to reflect on their own mortality over a sustained period of time tended to show shifts toward values of self-acceptance, intimacy, and community, and away from status-oriented values like money, image, and popularity.[20]

Irvin Yalom has studied several individuals who have confronted death and has noticed that this experience is highly transformative. He has seen death confrontation incite a rearrangement of life's priorities, a sense of liberation, an enhanced sense of living in the present, a vivid appreciation and acceptance of the elemental facts of life (changing seasons, falling leaves), deeper communication with loved ones, and fewer interpersonal fears.[21]

Let's explore our own mortality with openness, curiosity, deep reflection, humility, and self-compassion, and reflect on the legacy that we would like to leave behind so that we can start to live according to this legacy *right now.*

## PRACTICE

Spend some time in deep reflection, pondering the following questions:

- What does it mean to have a legacy? What might I want my legacy to be?
- What am I most proud of in my life thus far? What do I still wish to accomplish?
- What sorts of things do I say YES to in life? What do I say NO to?
- What roles do I play in my life that I most cherish? (Think about the various official or unofficial roles you play among family, friends, and work, in love, and so forth.) What roles do I still wish to play?
- What am I most passionate and enthusiastic about? (What's my *ikigai*?)
- What do I want my loved ones to say about me at the end of my life?
- How do I want my life to be honored or celebrated when I die?

Synthesize these reflections and write your own obituary (about one or two paragraphs). Think ahead to the end of your life, how you would like it to be, and how you would like to be remembered by those closest to you. Refrain from judging or censoring yourself. (You may wish to familiarize yourself with obituaries from your local newspaper if you are not familiar with the structure.)

## MY OBITUARY

Looking over what I wrote, am I on track?

- If I really were to die tomorrow, what would I regret not doing?
- How might I live my life differently, treat people differently, knowing that any of us could die tomorrow?
- How can I start living this legacy right this very moment?

## CHAPTER 8

# Become a Transcender

The great lesson from the true mystics—From the Zen monks,
and now also from the Humanistic and Transpersonal psychologists—
is that the sacred is in the ordinary, that it is to be found in one's
daily life, in one's neighbors, friends, and family, in one's back yard.

—Abraham Maslow,
*Religions, Values, and Peak-Experiences*

There are many ways to slice and dice the concept of transcendence. Indeed, Abraham Maslow gave thirty-five different conceptualizations of the term in a 1969 paper titled "Various Meanings of Transcendence."[1] In this chapter we will focus on a concept we call *healthy transcendence*, and we will help you cultivate more of it in your own life.

A lot of people these days are striving toward transcendence but are doing so without first building a healthy foundation. For instance, many people out there believe that a regimen of yoga and weekly meditation will somehow magically satisfy the other fundamental needs we've discussed throughout this book. As the creator of the mindfulness-based stress-reduction program (MBSR), Jon Kabat-Zinn, put it, "Wherever you go, there you are."[2] If one's need for self-esteem is woefully unsatisfied, for instance, that person will constantly be on the lookout for ways to satisfy the need, even if it involves pursuing "higher" spiritual practices.

Since the beginning of psychology itself, the field's founder, William James, pointed out the potential for spirituality to serve as a tool of self-enhancement, something we call "spiritual narcissism."[3] Indeed, many research studies have found that *any* skill that increases its centrality in our sense of self can breed a focus on self-enhancement. The principle is called the *self-centrality principle*, and paradoxically this also applies to the domain of self-transcendence! We can easily fool ourselves into thinking we are growing our whole self when in fact we are just growing our own ego. We call that *pseudo-transcendence*.[4]

So, what is *healthy* transcendence? Healthy transcendence is not about being more enlightened than others, but about being more *authentic* to ourselves and *synergistic* with the world. What is good for us is good for others. What we love to do, or that which we are even *called* to do, positively impacts others. There is a great connection between self and world. We don't choose ourselves over others, and we also don't choose others over ourselves. There is a harmonious integration between self and world. As Maslow said in one of his last public talks, it's as if our highest values and goals lie "equally outside and inside: therefore, [they have] transcended the geographical limitations of the self."[5]

Put another way, healthy transcendence is more horizontal than it is vertical. It's about confronting the realities of the human condition head-on with equanimity, wisdom, and loving-kindness and harnessing all that we are in the service of realizing the best version of ourself so we can help raise the bar for the whole of humanity.[6] With healthy transcendence, we have done the inner work to integrate our whole self, including our deprivation motivations, so that they no longer rule our actions in the world. We see the world on its own terms, and what we see may be intensely beautiful.

Many people don't know this, but toward the end of his life, Maslow proposed that transcendence is the highest human motivation, beyond self-actualization. He wrote that self-actualization is just a *bridge* to transcendence.[7] He was working on a "Theory Z," arguing that those who are guided in life by this worldview show "dichotomy-transcendence": they transcend black-and-white ways of seeing the world to see things that are seeming opposites (*e.g.*, good vs. evil, heart vs. head), as part of a larger whole of humanity.[8] He also argued that those guided by Theory Z are motivated by their "B-values" (or Being-values): the highest values that we get intrinsic satisfaction from meeting. His list of B-values included things such as the search for truth, goodness, beauty, justice, meaningfulness, playfulness, aliveness, excellence, simplicity, elegance, and wholeness.

Finally, Maslow argued that those motivated by Theory Z are seekers of "transcendent experiences." In transcendent experience individuals may be completely absorbed, experiencing rich perception; disorientation in physical time and space; ego-transcendence; a momentary loss of fears, anxiety, or inhibition; a heightened tendency for aestheticism, wonder, and surrender; and a fusion of themselves with the world.

Maslow called our capacity to find the miraculous in the everyday "plateau experiences" and argued that they are some of the strongest sources of transcendent experience. Indeed, not everything has to be a "peak experience," and we can often get so focused on chasing the highs that we miss out on the beauty that already exists all around us, and which we have seen many times before. We can experience these everyday transcendent experiences by embracing more savoring, gratitude, awe, and flow in our daily lives.

What did Maslow call these people who hold a Theory Z worldview? He called them *transcenders*. In this chapter we will help *you* become a transcender. As we catch the winds in our sails and begin to see the shorelines of growth in our lives, this final chapter is designed to guide you to experience the profound, the mystical, and that which unifies us in oneness with our fellow humankind and the universe. As positive existential psychologist Paul Wong and his colleagues put it, "It does not matter whether you live a privileged and luxurious life, or live in conditions of poverty or traumatic stress, all pathways leading to healing and flourishing involve the central mechanism of self-transcendence."[9]

Let's go.

# SAVOR LIFE

Happiness does not consist in things themselves
but in the relish we have of them.
—François de La Rochefoucald

In their foundational book, *Savoring: A New Model of Positive Experience*, Fred Bryant and Joseph Veroff introduce readers to the robust theory and science of savoring, what they call the "positive counterpart" to coping in life, which mediates the relationship between the objective conditions of a person's life and the degree to which we derive pleasure or fulfillment from those experiences.[10]

Savoring is the deliberate process of using thoughts, behaviors, and emotions to enhance the duration, intensity, and appreciation of positive experiences.[11] It is a potent mechanism by which we can actively transform positive experiences—even the simplest ones, like enjoying a cup of coffee, taking a hot shower, or a conversation with a friend—into positive states of being, and buffer against the negative impacts of anxiety, depression, and neuroticism.[12]

A wide body of research reveals that savoring is an important mechanism for deriving well-being from romantic relationships,[13] parent-child relationships,[14] and engagement with nature,[15] and even overcoming cancer and other potentially traumatic events.[16] Savoring has been shown to boost levels of happiness in individuals who experience few daily positive events,[17] predicts decreased depressive symptoms in older adults,[18] and is associated with higher levels of positive affect and life satisfaction in older adults and adolescents.[19]

For many of us, simply having a positive experience does not necessarily mean we will automatically take on positive emotions from it. This pathway requires focused attention, mindfulness, and meta-awareness[20]—an awareness of our own awareness—that may be cultivated with practice.

Savoring also requires us to recalibrate our ideas of what things in life will bring us the most joy and satisfaction. Human beings often tend to think that the big, monumental life events—this pandemic "ending," getting a massive raise at work, having a child, making that cross-country move—will yield the greatest boosts to our well-being. But far more important than these milestones (which reflect the *"I'll be happy when . . ."* syndrome we discussed in chapter 3) is simply making the most of opportunities for small, everyday happenings, and finding the pleasure, profundity, and complexity in seemingly ordinary moments.

We can savor events as they happen in real time: for example, finding a quiet moment of relief from the constant news cycle to take a bubble bath, taking an immersive hike, enjoying quality time with family and friends over a shared holiday meal, or tasting the fresh autumn air on our morning commute into the office. We can reminisce, or savor events that have happened in the past, such as looking back on a trip abroad, paging through a family photo album or an old yearbook, or reconnecting with an old friend from a former life. We can even savor events that have not happened yet! Through a process called *anticipation*, we can fantasize about the next vacation we will take or savor what it might feel like to attend that next live performance, imagining the feeling of the bass in our chest and allowing that collective feeling of singing and moving in the presence of thousands of strangers—and feeling at ease—permeate our being.

Read through the following statements, which are items from Dr. Bryant's Savoring Beliefs Inventory,[21] to determine your go-to temporal form of savoring. For each of the three categories (anticipating the future, savoring the present moment, reminiscing on the past), tally up the number of statements you agree with in the left column and the number of statements you disagree with in the right column. The greater the number of statements marked for each category, the more you tend toward savoring in this way.

| ANTICIPATING THE FUTURE | |
| --- | --- |
| *Agree:* | *Disagree:* |
| ❑ I get pleasure from looking forward. | ❑ I don't like to look forward too much. |
| ❑ I can feel the joy of anticipation. | ❑ Anticipating is a waste of time. |
| ❑ I can enjoy events before they occur. | ❑ I find it hard to get excited beforehand. |
| ❑ I can feel good by imagining an outcome. | ❑ I feel uncomfortable when I anticipate positive events. |

| SAVORING THE PRESENT MOMENT | |
| --- | --- |
| **Agree:** | **Disagree:** |
| ❑ I know how to make the most of a good time. | ❑ I find it hard to hold on to a good feeling. |
| ❑ I can prolong enjoyment by my own effort. | ❑ I am my own "worst enemy" in enjoying the moment. |
| ❑ I feel fully able to appreciate good things. | ❑ I can't seem to fully capture the joy of happy moments. |
| ❑ I find it easy to enjoy myself when I want to. | ❑ I don't enjoy things as much as I should. |
| **REMINISCING ON THE PAST** | |
| **Agree:** | **Disagree:** |
| ❑ I enjoy looking back on happy times. | ❑ I don't like to look back on happy times afterward. |
| ❑ I can feel good by remembering the past. | ❑ I feel disappointed when I reminisce. |
| ❑ I like to store memories for later recall. | ❑ Reminiscing is a waste of time. |
| ❑ I find it easy to rekindle joy from happy memories. | ❑ I find it best not to recall past fun times. |

Reflect:

- Of the three temporal forms of savoring (anticipating the future, savoring the present moment, reminiscing on the past), which type(s) am I most inclined to do naturally?
- When most recently have I savored in this way? What did I do?

In addition to the three temporal forms of savoring discussed above, Bryant and Veroff discuss four primary types of savoring processes that we encounter in our lives. Each of the types of savoring involves a focus of attention that is either *internal* (focused on the self) or *external* (focused on the world) and is either dominantly *cognitive* (involving thinking) or *experiential* (involving doing something). These four processes are summarized in the table on the next page.

| FOUR PRIMARY FORMS OF SAVORING[22] | | |
|---|---|---|
| | **INTERNAL SELF** | **EXTERNAL WORLD** |
| **Cognitive Reflection (Thinking)** | **Basking (pride)**<br><br>Being receptive to praise, pride, and congratulations<br><br>*For example: Enjoying the afterglow of cooking a fabulous meal or the satisfaction of cleaning your home, delivering an awesome presentation at work, contemplating one's fulfillment as a parent*<br><br>Negative counterpart: self-blame | **Thanksgiving (gratitude)**<br><br>Experiencing and expressing loving gratitude<br><br>*For example: Spending the afternoon with your mother and expressing gratitude that you have such a beautiful, close relationship; writing a note of gratitude to a teacher who inspired you on your career path; sharing gratitude for one thing each day at the dinner table*<br><br>Negative counterpart: grudge-holding |
| **Experiential Absorption (Doing)** | **Luxuriating (pleasure)**<br><br>Engaging the senses fully to an internally pleasurable experience<br><br>*For example: Enjoying a relaxing bubble bath or massage; slowly eating a meal, bite by bite; indulging in a glass of fine wine; luxuriating in intimate sexual contact*<br><br>Negative counterpart: suffering, pain/discomfort | **Marveling (awe)**<br><br>Losing yourself in the sublime grandeur, wonder, awe, and reverence of experience<br><br>*For example: Going outside during a thunderstorm to marvel at the sky's action, summiting to the top of a mountain and observing the Earth from above, gazing at the sky full of stars on a clear night, hiking through a forest of ancient redwood trees*<br><br>Negative counterpart: horror |

Reflect:

- Of the four types of savoring (basking, luxuriating, thanksgiving, and marveling), which type(s) am I most inclined to do naturally?
- When recently have I savored in this way? What did I do?

Bryant and Veroff provide insights into ten ways we might cultivate our ability to savor:[23]

STRATEGIES TO ENHANCE SAVORING

1. **Share with others.** Seeking out others to share our experiences with can augment our own positive emotions. We can tell a family member, partner, or friend how much we value the moment we are in, "infecting" our loved ones with appreciation. Make a ritual out of savoring a meal, an intimate moment, or any treasured shared experience.

2. **Actively build memories.** Actively pause and take what Bryant calls "mental photographs," or vivid memories that we store in our minds to return to later. No need to take out our phones; rather, these are images that we ingrain in our minds and say, "I want to remember this, and return to this moment later whenever I am stressed."

3. **Self-congratulate.** Many of us feel super-awkward reveling in our own glory because humility is a strength, and no one likes a braggart! However, we can slow down and let our hard work and success wash over us and share our accomplishments with others who can share in our joy. Celebrate small wins like setting healthy boundaries, and even failing gracefully!

4. **Sharpen your senses.** Slow down during pleasant activities to engage all of the senses we have access to: sight, smell, sound, touch, taste, proprioception (awareness of the movement of our bodies) and interoception (awareness of the sensations inside our bodies: our heartbeat, breathing, hunger, satiety, etc.). Eat and drink more slowly, taking in all the textures, flavors, and smells; attune to how a hot shower feels on our skin, how the water relaxes our muscles, and how the sound of running water has a calming effect on our mind and body.

5. **Use your body.** Jump for joy, laugh out loud, high-five (or elbow-tap or fist-bump) and dance with others to embrace positive events. Using our whole body facilitates deepening and spreading these experiences.

6. **Allow yourself to become fully absorbed.** While savoring requires periods of meta-awareness to actively detect and translate our positive experiences into positive emotions, we must also allow ourselves to just be one with our experiences, to get into flow, and lose ourselves. We may not want to interrupt a deep state of absorbed conversation at a dinner party by stopping mid-conversation to say, "How much fun is this party?!" Be mindful not to let well-intentioned attempts at savoring interrupt the mood.

7. **Rely on negative comparison.** Rather than constantly comparing ourselves to those who seem to have it all together, to our most ideal performances, or our highest strivings, we might compare ourselves to those who have less than we do, when times were worse, or what our lives would look like if we were bereft of our current fortune. We're all heard the expression "the grass is always greener on the other side." We believe that the grass is greener where *we water* it. We get to choose where we devote our attention.

8. **Count your blessings.** No matter where we are now, there is always something to be grateful for. Before we go naming all the things that are wrong about our current situation, we can instead focus on the blessings that are right in front of us. We might keep a gratitude journal or share our blessings with others to help us savor them.

9. **Avoid killjoy thinking.** Just as important as it is that we count our blessings, we can also use these blessings as ammunition to counteract our hardwired tendency to focus on the negative. Unfortunately, the negative things that happen can be really sticky for our brains, so it takes deliberate effort and attention to combat these basic, evolutionary instincts.

10. **Remember, it won't last forever.** Often the most precious and powerfully joyful moments of our lives are fleeting (it's part of what makes them so special). Knowing this, we can extract as much meaning and positive emotions from them

as possible and remember that even when they are over, we will always have them to reminisce and savor in the future.

## PRACTICE

1. **Create your own savoring ritual.** Set yourself up for a savoring experience using a temporal form and savoring type of your choice. Further, implement at least one strategy savoring-enhancing from the previous list. Some examples:
   - If you are a natural reminiscer and inclined toward thanksgiving, you might take out an old photo album and spend at least fifteen minutes paging through it, bringing a grateful awareness to this earlier time. Engage your child, partner, parent, or sibling to do it with you for your savoring strategy of sharing with others. You might even call up a relative who you come across to share gratitude with them.
   - If you are an anticipator and enjoy marveling, spend at least fifteen minutes imagining yourself on a trip somewhere you'd like to go in the future. Imagine yourself doing all the activities you'd like to do there (*e.g.*, sightseeing, taking beautiful hikes, sitting by the water and listening to the ocean). You can even pull up Google Earth and zoom in to this place, or search for images of this destination to visualize the landscape and feel immersed there from your own home. You may even feel inspired to start planning your trip! Allow yourself to be fully absorbed in this activity.
   - If you are most inclined to savor in the present moment and enjoy luxuriating, consider drawing yourself a bubble bath and spending at least fifteen minutes in the bath. Engage your body and all your senses fully; notice the smells, the sensations in your body, what happens to your breathing and heart rate from the calming sensations. Leave your phone in the other room or silence it except for relaxing music, lock the door, light some candles, and fully commit to luxuriating.

2. Allow savoring to become a regular practice that you incorporate into your daily routine for two weeks or more. Research shows that while there are no meaningful

differences in the benefits of different savoring interventions, the strength of effectiveness is related to the length of the intervention and the frequency![24] Additionally, it's important to engage in savoring activities that are most meaningful to us personally. There are no right or wrong ways to savor.

3. Reflect: How might embracing the positive through savoring practice equip me to be more present, focused, and able to engage in my daily life wholeheartedly and whole-mindedly? How might I pay some of these practices forward to help others around me?

# CULTIVATE GRATEFULNESS

Gratitude, I want to suggest,
is not only the best answer to the tragedies of life.
It is the best approach to life itself.
—Robert Solomon, *Spirituality for the Skeptic*

We hope by now it is clear that the practices in this book are designed to honor the totality of the human experience, and certainly not to embrace a positive outlook at all costs—what some psychologists refer to as "toxic positivity."[25] As gratitude researcher Robert Emmons points out, "To deny that life has its share of disappointments, frustrations, losses, hurts, setbacks, and sadness would be unrealistic and untenable. Life is suffering. No amount of positive thinking exercises will change this truth."[26]

The antidote to toxic positivity is tragic optimism, a phrase coined by the existential-humanistic psychologist and Holocaust survivor Viktor Frankl.[27] Tragic optimism involves the search for meaning amid the inevitable tragedies of human existence. As Robert Emmons and Robin Stern note, "True gratefulness rejoices in the other. Its ultimate goal is to reflect back the goodness that one has received by creatively seeking opportunities for giving."[28] These findings highlight the fact that gratitude can be a method of coping or "healing force."[29] Indeed, research shows that a number of positive mental health outcomes result from a regular gratitude practice, such as reduced lifetime risk for depression, anxiety, and substance use disorders.[30]

We posit that we can make use of our life challenges as a conduit to gratitude; to reconnect with the many basic advantages in our lives that we too often take for granted. As G. K. Chesterton put it, "Until we realize that things might not be, we cannot realize that things are." Indeed, several studies have found that people who have confronted life-threatening diseases report that their appreciation for life itself has increased and some of the most grateful people have gone through some of the most difficult experiences.[31]

Kristi Nelson, executive director of A Network for Grateful Living, personally faced her mortality at the age of thirty-three when she received a cancer diagnosis and underwent multiple surgeries, chemotherapy, and radiation. Nevertheless, she was constantly on the lookout for opportunities to cultivate gratefulness:

> I was in the hospital, separated from all my friends and family and tethered to all kinds of IVs and dealing with pain. And yet, I had nurses and technicians and doctors and cleaners who came into my room every single day. I remember thinking, what if this is my whole world now, what if this is all I have? And then I thought, I can always love these people.

Nelson makes a distinction between *gratitude*—a momentary feel-good, self-satisfying, reactive emotion—and *gratefulness*, an "overall orientation to life" that is "not contingent on something happening to us, but rather a way that we arrive to life."[32] Part of being human is that we will have a flicker of remembrance of our past suffering and then forget and start to take our current life for granted. But as Nelson notes, "The work is to remember more often than we forget."

# EXISTENTIAL GRATITUDE

Even in the mud and scum of things,
something always, always sings.
—Ralph Waldo Emerson

Lilian Jans-Beken and Paul Wong created an Existential Gratitude Scale to highlight the fact that we can have gratitude for *all* of human existence, not just the positive aspects. Read through the following items:

- I am grateful for my life even in times of suffering.
- I am grateful that my inner resources have increased as a result of overcoming adversities.
- I am grateful for the people in my life, even for those who have caused me much pain.
- I am thankful that I have something to live for, even though life has been very hard for me.
- I am grateful that every crisis represents an opportunity for me to grow.
- I have learned the importance of gratitude through suffering.

The researchers have found existential gratitude to be associated with "spiritual well-being" (the perception of an individual's spiritual quality of life), and that this association depends on the presence of symptoms of post-traumatic stress disorder (PTSD): the more symptoms, the stronger the relationship between existential gratitude and spiritual well-being. This is particularly critical, because it means that even in the presence of symptoms of a mental illness, growth and well-being are possible, perhaps even more possible! Suffering does not preclude growth, and it may actually catalyze it. This finding is also important considering that both gratitude and spirituality have been shown to be protective factors against anxiety and depression.[33]

Gratitude as an emotion can come and go, but gratefulness (or "existential gratitude") can pervade our entire existence. It asks for nothing, but is on the lookout to find the appreciation in everything. As Kristi Nelson put it, "Positive thinking says the glass is half-full. Dour thinking says it is half-empty. Gratitude helps us to better enjoy whatever is in the glass. But gratefulness can help us focus more intently on the radical fact of having a glass at all, making the most of the glass we have, and on ensuring that those around us have a glass as well."[34]

# PRACTICE

Read each statement and consider to what extent you agree with them:

- I am resentful that life has treated me unfairly.
- I wish that I had never been born.
- I still feel bitter for all the bad experiences that have happened to me.

Research has found that these items are strongly negatively associated with existential gratitude.[35] In other words, those who agree with these items tend to have *less* existential gratitude. Life is suffering. That is a given of existence.[36]

Other bodies of research show that narcissism and cynicism are strong inhibitors of gratitude and have been called "thieves of thankfulness."[37] Even after controlling for initial levels of gratitude, narcissism and cynicism interact in a vicious cycle and are negatively associated with gratefulness over time.

Reflect:

1. While I may not feel grateful for some of the awful things that have happened to me, how might I reframe some of my negative life experiences? Instead of feeling resentment toward them, how might I lean in to the ways these experiences have made me stronger, wiser, more compassionate, and whole as a human being?
   - What inner resources have increased within me?
   - How have I grown from the pain I've experienced?
   - In what ways am I still growing?
   - What values have become more important to me since my suffering?

2. Instead of feeling entitled to happiness and a life completely free of suffering, or even cynically expecting everything to always go wrong, in what ways can I harness more existential gratitude for the inevitable twists and turns of human existence? In what ways might I appreciate that I have a container of human experience in the first place, without focusing on whether it's half full or half empty?

3. Please read the following passage, created by Philip Cozzolino and his colleagues:

> *Imagine that you are visiting a friend who lives on the twentieth floor of an old downtown apartment building. It's the middle of the night, when you are suddenly awakened from a deep sleep by the sound of screams and the choking smell of smoke. You reach over to the nightstand and turn on the light. You are shocked to find the room filling fast with thick clouds of smoke. You run to the door and reach for the handle. You pull back in pain as the intense heat of the knob scalds you violently. Grabbing a blanket off the bed and using it as protection, you manage to turn the handle and open the door. Almost immediately, a huge wave of flame and smoke roars into the room, knocking you back and literally off your feet. There is no way to leave the room. It is getting very hard to breathe, and the heat from the flames is almost unbearable. Panicked, you scramble to the only window in the room and try to open it. As you struggle, you realize the old window is virtually painted shut around all the edges. It doesn't budge. Your eyes are barely open now, filled with tears from the smoke. You try calling out for help, but the air to form the words is not there. You drop to the floor, hoping to escape the rising smoke, but it is too late. The room is filled top to bottom with thick fumes and nearly entirely in flames. With your heart pounding, it suddenly hits you, as time seems to stand still, that you are literally moments away from dying. The inevitable unknown that was always waiting for you has finally arrived. Out of breath and weak, you shut your eyes and wait for the end.*

- Describe in detail the thoughts and emotions you felt while imagining the scenario.
- If you did experience this event, how do you think you would handle the final moments?

- After imagining that this did happen to you, describe the life you led up to that point.
- How do you feel your family would react if this did happen to you?

The "death reflection" scenario was created by Philip Cozzolino and his colleagues to contrast with other scenarios in which people have "mortality salience," or simply become aware of their death.[38] The researchers found that this death reflection exercise generated intrinsic, unselfish behavior, whereas mortality salience in some cases actually led to increased greed! Other research has found that people randomly assigned to engage in this death reflection exercise showed increased gratitude for their lives compared to participants who were randomly asked to imagine waking up to "begin another typical day."[39] Therefore, there seems to be value in this sort of deeper reflection.

# WAKE UP GRATEFUL

When we wake up in the morning and experience a sense of gratefulness just for the fact of being alive, with our heart and senses open to the gifts and opportunities of another day, it's a more radical approach to gratitude that's not contingent on something happening to us, but rather a way that we arrive to life.
—Kristi Nelson[40]

Every morning before author Stephen King gets out of bed at 6 a.m., he makes a mental note of all the things he is grateful for: "It's a nice way to start the day because you get a chance to almost do a review of your current life, your current status." It's easy to take for granted the most enduring yet most essential aspects of our existence.

## PRACTICE

Kristi Nelson suggests the following gratefulness practice every morning: "When you wake up in the morning, before you even get out of bed, pause to think of five things you're grateful for. It could be: *My lungs are breathing. The air temperature is comfortable. I had an interesting dream. My eyes can open. I get to put my feet on the floor and walk out of the room. There are people I love. I'm still here.* You're calling forth those things that you don't have to do anything to earn, and that remind you that this day is a gift."[41]

You may write these down in your journal or in a note on your phone; discuss them with a friend, colleague, or partner; or simply meditate on them quietly.

# PROSPECTIVE GRATITUDE

## PRACTICE

If you are struggling with feeling gratitude in your current situation, project yourself into the future and imagine how grateful you will be when your circumstances change. Reflect: On a scale of 1 (not at all) to 7 (extremely), rate the degree to which you anticipate feeling grateful in the future, two to three months from now. What about this experience might you be grateful for?

Robert Emmons has found that this exercise has been very powerful for people during the COVID-19 pandemic. As he told Scott in personal correspondence, "This way of thinking has offered a fresh perspective on what it means to choose gratefulness no matter what is happening in one's life. It's a defiant attitude that insists that gratitude is the best approach to life, no matter what. The elasticity of gratitude allows us to be grateful for the past, present, and what is still to come. Few emotions have such a long arc."

# FIND FLOW

The best moments in our lives are not the passive, receptive,
relaxing times . . . The best moments usually occur if a person's body
or mind is stretched to its limits in a voluntary effort to
accomplish something difficult and worthwhile.
—Mihály Csíkszentmihály, 1990

Can you remember a time recently when you felt deeply "in the zone"? When you were so immersed in what you were doing that you lost track of time and used all your mental capacity—thoughts, feelings, and intentions—to focus on a single goal? Perhaps you were so deeply lost in the activity that your actions and awareness were completely one; you may have forgotten to eat or use the bathroom and, dare we say, left your phone somewhere far away . . . in other words, you were unaware of yourself.[42]

Note, we're talking states of *active* engagement here, not simply scrolling on social media or binge-watching *The Great British Bake Off.* Meditate on this for a moment and try to recall an activity that has brought you into this state of being, termed by the legendary late psychologist Mihály Csíkszentmihályi as "flow."[43]

Typically, we enter flow when we are doing things that are *intrinsically motivated*: something that we do for its own sake, because we love it (you likely find flow in your *ikigai*)! The challenge at hand must be matched by an adequate level of skill; we are not so aroused or overwhelmed that our bodies sense danger and put us into fight-or-flight mode, and we're also not such masters that we dominate the task and veer into boredom. We must also know the "rules" of the game, so that we get some sort of feedback on how we're doing. Finally, we must be fully immersed; we cannot get into flow when we are mired in distraction and disturbance.

By fully delving into an activity and out of our heads, we have no psychic energy left to self-scrutinize; we may find that our self-consciousness fades away. We can find flow on our own as well as in groups when we harmonize with others through mutual tasks. Often, finding flow involves challenging our bodies and minds to their limits; striving to accomplish something new, difficult, or worthwhile; and discovering rewards in the process of each moment. Sonja Lyubomirsky describes eight tools for enhancing flow, which we summarize below.[44]

# PRACTICE

| | |
|---|---|
| **Control Our Attention** | One of the greatest barriers to flow is a loss of our attention toward lower-value, lower-quality tasks (such as answering email or texts!). Craft your environment to optimize your attention on tasks that matter. Silence your cellphone (or put it in another room entirely), turn off notification alarms, and minimize distractions wherever possible. |
| **Open Ourselves to New Experiences** | Be open to new and different experiences, such as going camping, playing a new sport, traveling to a foreign place, or trying new types of cuisine. When we continue to challenge ourselves, we avoid becoming complacent in an overly routinized life. |
| **Be Lifelong Learners** | Learning and embracing new challenges throughout the course of life is critical for finding flow when we've already mastered many skills. We can keep pushing ourselves with new goals at any age. |
| **Learn What Flows** | We may get into flow or have great potential for flow but just fail to recognize it. Pay close attention and establish precise time periods and activities during which we are in flow and try to amplify these activities (and deliberately eliminate distractions). |
| **Transform Routine Tasks** | We can find "micro-flow" states even in mundane activities, such as exercise, errands, waiting for a train, cleaning, or sitting in class or a meeting. Transform routine tasks by deliberately turning up our engagement, like setting new challenges, writing songs or poems in our heads, gamifying chores, taking notes, or brainstorming new ways of doing things. |
| **Flow in Conversation** | Develop goals within conversations to learn more about the person we're speaking with: What is on her mind? What emotions is she experiencing? Have I learned something about her that I didn't know before? Focus our full attention on the speaker and on our reactions to her words. Prompt with follow-up questions: "And then what happened?" "Why did you think that?" |
| **Engage in Smart Leisure** | Consider making leisure time "smarter" by engaging in activities in which we use our minds fully on the task at hand; for example, rather than multitasking, like watching TV as we cook, put on music and tune in to the ingredients and flavors. |

| Engage in Smart Work | Cater the tasks we need to do at work to align with our skills, passions, and values. Do our tasks without distraction, and devote specific time every hour to answering emails or messages if possible, rather than allowing them to trickle in and interrupt flow. |
| --- | --- |

1. Start by reflecting on a previous flow experience you've had. Perhaps this was a time when you were completely absorbed, with a substantial shift of self-consciousness and perception of time, in which you were at one with an activity. Consider what factors facilitated this experience. Were you by yourself or with others? What factors, if any, may have impeded the experience? Consider how you might solve the potential obstacles to flow.

2. Next, go flow! Intentionally set yourself up for a flow experience, considering the facilitators and barriers you've experienced in the past.

3. After you've completed your flow experience, reflect on the following:
   - What did I do?
   - How did it go? What worked to induce flow? What didn't work?
   - How did it feel in the moment to experience flow? How did I feel afterward?
   - Is there anyone I shared this experience with? Is there anyone I might share this experience with next time?
   - How might I incorporate more flow into my life on a regular basis?

# EXPERIENCE AWE

Our colleague and friend David Yaden, who studies spiritual experiences, has referred to awe as "the everyperson's spiritual experience."[45] Whereas only about one-third of people perceive that they have had a profound awakening that has changed the direction of their life, nearly everyone has experienced awe: that wondrous and humbling emotion comprising ecstasy and deep reverence, when our consciousness feels vast, we struggle to mentally process and integrate the experience, time perception changes, our sense of self is diminished, our feeling of connectedness with other people and the environment heightens, and our skin becomes enveloped in goose bumps.[46]

In other words, we experience awe for things so grand that we have trouble fully comprehending them. For example, we may feel awe in the presence of natural marvels such as large mountains, vast oceans, clear starry skies, canyons, waterfalls, or majestic large animals; among masterful art, performance, or architecture; ancient civilizations; or through religious, spiritual, or meditative experiences. Research reveals many positive outcomes associated with awe experiences, including enhanced life satisfaction,[47] a feeling that there is more time available to experience the world,[48] increased helping behaviors and generosity toward others,[49] and decreased aggressive attitudes.[50] What's more is that we don't even have to experience these awe-inspiring scenes firsthand or up close to reap the benefits; even photos or videos can suffice, which means that awe is accessible to any of us with an internet connection.

## PRACTICE

1. Start by reflecting on a time in the past that you experienced intense awe. This can be from any time in your life, but recent enough that you remember the details vividly. Consider what specifically facilitated this experience of awe. In other words, what features of the experience induced a sense of ecstasy or reverence within you? Features might include vastness (being in the presence of something grand), a need for accommodation (or feeling challenged to mentally process the experience), a distortion of time, self-diminishment (feeling metaphysically tiny in the large universe), connectedness (having the sense of being connected to everything around you), or specific physical sensations (goose bumps, jaw drop, a chill down your spine, etc.).

2. Next, intentionally set yourself up for an awe experience, to the best of your ability. This can be anything that excites you and feels accessible to you: watching a video online of a natural landscape, waking up early to watch the sunrise, stargazing, taking a nature walk or hike somewhere beautiful, going to a museum, or even watching

a live performance that touches you. Go out and complete this activity, paying close attention, with minimal distraction, allowing yourself to be completely immersed. Try to engage your senses fully and savor this awe experience.

3. After you complete your awe activity, reflect on the following:
   - What did I choose to do?
   - How did it feel in the moment? How did it feel afterward?
   - Is there anyone I'd like to share this awe experience with?
   - How might I incorporate more awe into my life on a regular basis?

# "YES, AND . . ." LIFE

One of the main motivations of a transcender, according to Maslow, is "dichotomy-transcendence," or the drive to transcend everyday false binaries we hold and see them as parts of a larger integrate whole of humanity. There are a lot of dichotomies we might hold in our minds: male vs. female, heart vs. head, lust vs. love, good vs. evil, national vs. global, individual vs. collective, selfish vs. unselfish, kindness vs. ruthlessness, happy vs. sad, mystical vs. realistic, and the list goes on . . . What would it look like to view these not as opposites, but as complementary parts of a larger whole? Dichotomy transcendence is core to wisdom, and the transcender can be thought of as having a wise perspective on life. As clinical psychologist Deirdre Kramer put it,

> Wise people have learned to view the positive and negative and synthesize them to create a more human, more integrated sense of self, in all its frailty and vulnerability . . . They seem able to first embrace and then transcend self-concerns to integrate their capacity for introspection with a deep and abiding concern for human relationships and generative concern for others.[51]

In this final practice, we will help you cultivate this way of thinking using a well-known improv technique called "yes, and . . . ," or, as improv veteran Anne Libera likes to call it, "explore and heighten."[52] Improv is a form of live theater in which characters generate a scene together in the moment. It requires thinking fast on one's feet and working together as a team to support each other and continually heighten possibilities in the conversation with spontaneity and fun. Wouldn't it be great if we could cultivate more of this way of being in our daily lives and have a bit more of what Maslow referred to as "healthy childishness"—integrating the spontaneous wonder of childhood with the wisdom of adulthood?

The ethos of "yes, and" is an important lesson in exploring apparent contradictions in our lives—both interpersonally and intrapersonally within ourselves as we experience inner conflict or ambivalence. In her master's capstone on the topic, *"Yes And": Exploring and Heightening the Positive Psychology in Improvisation*, professional improviser Bridget Erica Elam describes "yes, and" as a "mantra that encapsulates almost every element of being an excellent individual improv performer, an excellent improv teammate, and an excellent human."[53]

"Yes," Elam says, is "awareness, acceptance, and appreciation." "Yes" indicates, "I hear what you are saying; I see where you are coming from. I want to engage with you further." Note, it's not necessarily *"I agree with exactly what you are saying."* It is instead a recognition of a starting place, a foundation on which to build the rest of the scene. "And," she says, is "agency, autonomy, and action." Through the "and," we build a cohesive story with our stage partner, accepting the reality that our scene partner has established, and building on it by adding our own perspective and spin to that reality.

Elam provides the following stage example:[54]

*If I begin the scene by saying, "Mom, no one is ever gonna ask me to the prom," and you respond with, "I'm not your mom, I'm a blender" (and then begin spinning in a circle while making whirring sounds), you have just said "no" to my initiation. However, if you respond, "Sweetie, of course they will!" you are accepting the circumstances I have initiated—namely, that I am your child, you are my mom, and the prom is coming up. Notice you didn't agree with me, but you did accept my initiation, thereby saying "yes" to me.*

*The "and" in "yes and" is your opportunity to contribute. If "Sweetie, of course they will!" is the "yes" then you can add value by building upon what has been established and heightening it in a multitude of ways. "Sweetie, of course they will! You're the prettiest girl in school" or "Sweetie, of course they will! Your father is the President of the United States" or "Sweetie, of course they will! Mama's been slogging over this hot cauldron all afternoon and I've put a spell on the entire senior class." Anything you add that builds upon what has already been established gives your scene partner something to explore and heighten.*

Notably, the "yes, and" rule can help us acknowledge one another's truths and hold multiple possibilities and perspectives at the same time. To be clear, our intention in illustrating this fundamental principle of improv is not necessarily to train you as improvisers or to inspire you all to go to your local comedy club and sign up for classes (though we certainly encourage that if you are so inclined—what a way to open your sail!). We primarily elicit the microcosm of improv to illustrate the power that "yes, and" may hold for us off the stage in the real world.

In daily life we often fall subject to the defense of "splitting" or resort to "all-or-nothing" thinking (remember the cognitive distortions? See chapter 3 for a refresher). However, making room for uncertainty by practicing "yes, and" with ourselves and others can help us honor the complexity and richness of our full human experience, and not only tolerate but embrace and revel in the complexities, contradictions, and gray areas we live in.

This idea is at the core of a form of cognitive therapy called Dialectical Behavioral Therapy (DBT) developed by Marsha Linehan, which helps individuals embrace two seemingly opposite high-level treatment goals: *self-acceptance* ("Yes, I am doing my very best") and *change* ("And I know that I have much room to grow"). The "dialectic" in DBT honors that two ideas that may seem to contradict one another on the surface can both be true at the same time. DBT encourages clients to veer away from "yes, *but . . .*" language, which undermines one part of the experience in favor of another, recapitulating a black-and-white view of the world. Whereas "yes, but . . ." narrows the possibilities and places conflicting experiences and views at odds with one another, "yes, and" helps us to enthusiastically accept the totality of an experience; validate, rather than undermine conflicting impulses or feelings; and thereby foster mutual, positive regard with ourselves and others.

Here are some examples of how we can embrace the notion of "yes, and" (as opposed to "yes, but . . .") with ourselves as we process and digest our own ambivalence. Think about how these sentences might sound and how we might take away a different meaning if the word *but* were used instead of *and*.

- *Yes:* Working from home has been a gift in so many ways, I have had the ability to spend more time with my family, *and:* I have really struggled with setting boundaries between work and home life and look forward to getting back to the office.
- *Yes:* I treasure being a parent and find so much meaning and joy from my children and watching them grow, *and:* homeschooling them has been taxing, exhausting, and I feel totally out of my league. I need a break.
- *Yes:* I respect and value my boss, *and:* I would feel more supported by her if we had more frequent check-ins and face-to-face time.

We invite you to come up with some of your own "Yes, and" phrases to honor any ambivalence you may be feeling right now.

Yes:

And:

Yes:

And:

Yes:

And:

# PRACTICE

1. Think about a few recent experiences that brought up strong feelings for you, perhaps mixed feelings, or ambivalence (such as in the situations just provided). In writing, or in conversation with a partner or group, reflect on your ambivalence, and the variety of the feelings that have come up for you. As you're writing or speaking, monitor yourself—or ask others to monitor you—for the word *but* or any of its close cousins like *however*, *yet*, *nonetheless*, etc. Analyze how you use these words and if instead the word *and* might be more appropriate to explore and heighten each part of the whole experience.

2. Reflect on your reflection (meta-reflection):
   - How might I tend to oversimply my processing of certain experiences in favor of only part of a false dichotomy?
   - Why might it be simpler for me to pay attention to only some aspects of an experience instead of the whole?
   - How might I be more intentional about embracing the gray areas of life, even when it feels uncomfortable or uncertain?

3. Begin to pay attention to conversations that you have with others and notice when the word *but* comes up. Of course, there are times when *but* is appropriate, particularly if we are trying to negate part of an experience. Notice when you or others might be using *but* inappropriately, for example, when two ideas might both be true at the same time. Vow to call this in, bringing "yes, and" to the forefront of your life.

# Community Actualization

C ongratulations on making it to the very final section of the workbook! Hopefully by now you are well acquainted with your boat: the security needs that make up the base and the growth needs that make up your sail. Perhaps you have begun the process of accepting your whole self, finding ways to welcome and integrate your dark sides, facing that which scares you, and saying "yes, and . . ." to the complex feelings that arise along the way.

You may also be experimenting with treating yourself and others with greater kindness, embracing forgivingness, and giving of yourself—and asking for the help of others—in ways that are more effective, authentic, and gratifying. You might be extracting greater positive emotions and plateau experiences from your daily routines and may even be contemplating how to reorient your life to devote more attention and time toward those causes, people, and values that matter most to you.

Now, before we send you back to start the journey all over again with the new perspectives and insights that you've gained on this first voyage—remember, growth is a lifelong, nonlinear process—we'd like to help you refuel, step off your own boat, and critically, take stock of the other boats around you and the waters we are all in.

*Growth is a lifelong, nonlinear process.*

As we've noted, healthy transcendence emerges from the integration of the whole self *in service of realizing the good of society.* As the very wise authors and partners

Isaac and Ora Prilleltensky posit, our ability to transcend in this way teeters greatly on the waters we are in: namely, whether we are part of a "Me Culture" or a "We Culture."[1] The former, which is playing out as the dominant narrative in the U.S. throughout the COVID-19 pandemic, assumes *I have the right to feel valued and happy.* The Prilleltenskys juxtapose this with the ameliorative "We Culture" that supposes, yes, and . . . *"We all have the right and responsibility to feel valued and add value, to self, and others, so that we may all experience wellness and fairness."*[2] As Isaac Prilleltensky notes, this communitarianism philosophy "holds the tension between rights and responsibilities, between feeling valued and adding value, between wellness and fairness, and between freedom and community."[3] It's not about one or the other, but about "yes, and!" After all, group narcissism can be just as detrimental as hyperindividualism.[4]

Justifying our need for a "We Culture," the Prilleltenskys astutely claim that the greatest ills in our society—discrimination, oppression, inequity, rising rates of mental illness and suicide, indifference to environmental catastrophe, and the rise of authoritarianism, nationalism, and divisive movements around the world—will not be thwarted when only *individuals* become enlightened. Rather, these opportunities for healing require collective, societal, and structural action.[5]

A great example of a "We Culture" comes from the ancient wisdom of indigenous people.[6] In 1938, Maslow spent six weeks living among the northern Blackfoot Nation on the Siksika reserve in Alberta, Canada, studying and marveling at their way of life.[7] The Blackfoot aim to leave no one behind, and the wealthiest person in their culture is the one who has almost nothing left because they have given it all away.[8] They consider it a *community responsibility* to ensure that everyone's basic needs are met and to create the conditions that allow each person to live their purpose and fulfill their full potential.[9]

Cindy Blackstock, executive director of the First Nations Child and Family Caring Society of Canada, refers to this indigenous wisdom as "community actualization."[10] What's more, this focus on communal cooperation is not done only for the current generation to prosper but so that there can be "cultural perpetuity"; each generation sees it as their responsibility to pass on their tribe's values and communal wisdom to future generations. As Blackstock notes, "First Nations often consider their actions in terms of the impacts of the 'seven generations.' This means that one's actions are informed by the experience of the past seven generations and by considering the consequences for the seven generations to follow."[11]

The COVID-19 pandemic has affected us all, making us realize that while we're each in our own boats traveling in our own individual directions, we really are inextricably connected to and interdependent on one another. Our own actions, even within our own boats, have rippling effects, creating tides and wakes that impact those around us as well as those who will come after us. We've seen waves crashing down at all of us at once, and at the same time, we've also witnessed vast inequalities.

What an opportunity not only for post-pandemic *personal* growth but also for growth as a society. As Teju Ravilochan, founder of GatherFor, notes, it might be time to put away our old stories about how the world works and embrace new stories about how we live and how we can help. Deeply influenced by indigenous wisdom, Ravilochan writes,

> *This is our moment to step out of our lonely struggle to fend for ourselves, a story maintained by those winning in the status quo. This is our moment not to create something new, but to return to an ancient way of being, known to the Blackfoot, the Lakota, the Natives of the Cheyenne River Territory, and other First Nations. It's a story that leaves no one without a family: a story in which we begin by offering each other belonging, and continue by teaching our descendants how we lived: together.[12]*

We hope the practices in this book help you to become more fully human so that you can be in a better position to exist in this world harmoniously and synergistically, where helping yourself also helps raise the tide for everyone.

Bon voyage.

# NOTES FOR REFLECTION

## ACKNOWLEDGMENTS

This book would not have been possible without the unceasing support of our families—including our incredibly supportive parents—for being our biggest cheerleaders, role models, and exemplars of growth throughout the lifespan. For Scott, much love to Barbara and Michael Kaufman, and for Jordyn, much love goes to Michele and Stephen Feingold, and Jordyn's sister, Amanda Kornhauser. There are no words to sufficiently thank Jordyn's husband, Ira Schlosberg, for being by her side every step of writing this book and growing with her for the last seven years, embracing the Michelangelo phenomenon, and treating her with unconditional positive regard every day. I love you, Ira.

Thank you to Jordyn's mentors at the Icahn School of Medicine at Mount Sinai: Antonia New, Asher Simon, Dennis Charney, Jacob Appel, Jacqueline Hargrove, Jonathan Ripp, Laurie Keefer, and the entire Office of Medical Education, the Department of Psychiatry, and the Office of Well-Being and Resilience, for investing in and guiding Jordyn to become an outstanding clinician, researcher, and teacher; to the leadership of the University of Pennsylvania's Master of Applied Positive Psychology program: James Pawelski, Leona Brandwene, Martin Seligman, and the MAPP alumni community, for igniting her passion to bridge the gaps between health and sustainable well-being; to her colleagues and collaborators Annie Hart, Carly Kaplan, Greg Wallingford, Halley Kaye-Kauderer, and Sanj Katyal for co-teaching, authoring, imagining, and creating the future of positive medicine. To 14F, for humoring her for four years of medical school and for embracing positive medicine and transcendence in their home and practices. Of course, Jordyn thanks her dear friend and coauthor SBK, for his incredible partnership and teamwork, for teaching her what it means to write a book, for constantly inspiring her and believing in her dreams, and, most importantly, for his friendship.

Scott would like to return the gratitude to Jordyn. It has been a true delight watching her growth journey over the years; this book is just the start of a wondrous and productive career. Scott would also like to thank the many collaborators, mentors, podcast guests, and friends he has had over the years who have made this book possible. The many conversations over the years on *The Psychology Podcast* have immensely influenced the research and ideas presented in this book. During the writing of this book, he would like to single out Krista Stryker, Clare Sarah Goodridge, and Alice Wilder for their immense support, friendship, and encouragement to keep choosing the growth option. Their constant positive encouragement has inspired him to help others self-actualize and transcend.

Together, Scott and Jordyn would like to explicitly thank Andra Gailis, Anne Libera, Arthur Brooks, Eranda Jayawide, Kelly Leonard, Pauline Rose Clance, Reece Brown, Rephael Houston, Ryan Niemiec, and Shayna Schlosberg for their wisdom, brainstorming, and guidance through the development of this important book.

Finally, a heartfelt thank-you to our agent James Levine, our editor Marian Lizzi, and copyeditor Amy Brosey for helping us bring this book to life.

# NOTES

## Introduction

1. Yalom, I. D. (1980). *Existential psychotherapy*. New York: Basic Books.
2. Cooban, A. (2021, July 7). *95% of workers are thinking about quitting their jobs, according to a new survey—and burnout is the number one reason*. Insider. https://www.businessinsider.com /labor-shortage-workers-quitting-quit-job-pandemic-covid-survey-monster-2021-7.
3. Richter, F. (2022, January 11). *The Great Resignation*. Statista Infographics. https://www.statista .com/chart/26186/number-of-people-quitting-their-jobs-in-the-united-states/.
4. Bonanno, G. (2021). *The end of trauma: How the new science of resilience is changing how we think about PTSD*. New York: Basic Books.
5. Bonanno, G. (2021). *The end of trauma: How the new science of resilience is changing how we think about PTSD*. New York: Basic Books.
6. Witters, D., & Agrawal, S. (2021, July 7). *Americans' Life Ratings Reach Record High*. Gallup.com. https://news.gallup.com/poll/351932/americans-life-ratings-reach-record-high.aspx?fbclid =IwAR3w8G6La671GQ9DPeTmx3jf6FEYkYDp0AGCGGW8aMLOjJS8zUmdxP6bZck.
7. Watkins, P. W., Emmons, R., Amador, T., & Gromfin, D. (2021). Growth of gratitude in times of trouble: Gratitude in the pandemic. *International Positive Psychology World Congress*. https:/doi .org/10.13140/RG.2.213815.34722.
8. Campbell, J. (1949). *The hero with a thousand faces* (1st ed.). Princeton: Princeton University Press.
9. Tedeschi, R., Shakespeare-Finch, J., Taku, K., & Calhoun, L. G. (2018). *Posttraumatic growth: theory, research, and applications*. New York: Routledge.
10. Yalom, I. D. (1980). *Existential psychotherapy*. New York: Basic Books.
11. Yalom, I. D. (2009). *Staring at the sun: Overcoming the terror of death*. San Francisco: Jossey-Bass.
12. We acknowledge that perception is not always the same as actuality. Self-perceived changes in creativity may not accompany real changes in creative thinking. However, we still believe even shifts in perception can have a profound impact on people's lives.
13. Wagner, L., & Gander, F. (2021, November 1). *Did the COVID-19 pandemic make us better people?* The EJP Blog. https://www.ejp-blog.com/blog/2021/11/1/did-the-covid-19-pandemic-make-us -better-people.
14. Bloom, P. (2021). *The sweet spot: The pleasures of suffering and the search for meaning*. New York: Ecco.
15. Bloom, P. (2021). *The sweet spot: The pleasures of suffering and the search for meaning*. New York:

Ecco; Kjærgaard, A., Leon, G. R., & Venables, N. C. (2014). The "right stuff" for a solo sailboat circumnavigation of the globe. *Environment and Behavior*, 1–25; Kjærgaard, A., Leon, G. R., Venables, N. C., & Fink, B. A. (2017). Personality, personal values and growth in military special unit patrol teams operating in a polar environment. *Military Psychology, 25,* 13–22; Smith, N., Kinnafick, F., Cooley, S. J., & Sandal, G. M. (2016). Reported growth following mountaineering expeditions: The role of personality and perceived stress. *Environment and Behavior*, 1–23; Suedfeld, P., Legkaia, K., & Brcic, J. (2010). Changes in the hierarchy of value references associated with flying in space. *Journal of Personality, 78,* 1411–1435.

16. Tedeschi, R. G., & Moore, B. A. (2016). *The posttraumatic growth workbook: Coming through trauma wiser, stronger, and more resilient.* Oakland: New Harbinger Publications.

17. Keyes, C. L. M. (2002). The mental health continuum: From languishing to flourishing in life. *Journal of Health and Social Behavior, 32,* 207–222; Grant, A. (2021). There's a name for the blah you're feeling: It's called languishing. *The New York Times.* https://www.nytimes.com/2021/04/19/well/mind/covid-mental-health-languishing.html.

18. Jayawickreme, E., Infurna, F. J., Alajak, K., Blackie, L. E. R., Chopik, W. J., . . . Zonneveld, R., et al. (2021). Post-traumatic growth as positive personality change: Challenges, opportunities, and recommendations. *Journal of Personality, 89,* 145–165; Mangelsdorf, J., Eid, M., & Luhmann, M. (2018). Does growth require suffering? A systematic review and meta-analysis on genuine posttraumatic and postecstatic growth. *Psychological Bulletin, 145,* 302–338.

19. Roepke, A. M. (2013). Gains without pains? Growth after positive events. *Journal of Positive Psychology, 8,* 280–291.

20. Horney, K. (1959). *Neurosis and human growth.* New York: W. W. Norton; Kaufman, S. B. (2021). *Transcend: The new science of self-actualization.* New York: TarcherPerigee.

21. Rogers, C. R. (1961). *On becoming a person: A therapist's view of psychotherapy.* New York: Houghton Mifflin.

22. Kaufman, S. B. (2021). *Transcend: The new science of self-actualization.* New York: TarcherPerigee.

23. Ravilochan, T. (2021, April 4). *Could the Blackfoot wisdom that inspired Maslow guide us now?* Medium. https://gatherfor.medium.com/maslow-got-it-wrong-ae45d6217a8c.

24. Ravilochan, T. (2021, April 4). *Could the Blackfoot wisdom that inspired Maslow guide us now?* Medium. https://gatherfor.medium.com/maslow-got-it-wrong-ae45d6217a8c.

25. Horney, K. (1945). *Our inner conflicts: A constructive theory of neurosis.* New York: W. W. Norton.

**Chapter 1: Anchor Yourself**

1. Kaufman, S. B. (2021). *Transcend: The new science of self-actualization.* New York: TarcherPerigee.

2. Kaufman, S. B. (2021). *Transcend: The new science of self-actualization.* New York: TarcherPerigee; also see Bridgman, T., Cummings, S., & Ballard, J. (2019). Who built Maslow's pyramid? A history of the creation of management studies' most famous symbol and its implications for management education. *Academy of Management Learning & Education, 18,* https:/doi.org/10.5465/amle.2017.0351.

3. Drigotas, S. M. (2002). The Michelangelo phenomenon and personal well-being. *Journal of Personality, 70,* 59–77.

4. Schwartz, C. E., & Sendor, M. (1999). Helping others helps oneself: Response shift effects in peer support. *Social Science and Medicine, 48,* 1563–1575; Rebele, R. W. (2015). Being "otherish": Resolving the false choice between personal and prosocial goals. In R. J. Burke, K. M. Page, & C. L. Cooper (eds.), *Flourishing in life, work, and careers: Individual wellbeing and career experience* (pp. 26–44). New Horizons in Management. Cheltenham, UK: Edward Elgar Publishing.

5. Porges, S. W. (2011). *The polyvagal theory: Neurophysiological foundations of emotions, attachment, communication, and self-regulation.* New York: W. W. Norton.

6. Porges, S. W. (2016). Trauma and the Polyvagal Theory: a commentary. *International Journal of Multidisciplinary Trauma Studies, 1,* 24–30. https://doi.org/10.3280/ijm2016-001003.

7. Author, counselor, and trauma expert Resmaa Menakem writes extensively about this vagal pathway in his outstanding book, *My grandmother's hands: Racialized trauma and the pathway to mending our hearts and bodies.* Menakem discusses the idea that our bodies, not our brains, are truly the center of race-based trauma. He writes, "In the aftermath of a highly stressful event, our lizard brain may embed a reflexive trauma response—a wordless story of danger—in our body. This trauma can cause us to react to present events in ways that seem out of proportion or wildly inappropriate to what's actually going on." Menakem, R. (2021). *My grandmother's hands: Racialized trauma and the pathway to mending our hearts and bodies.* New York: Penguin Books, 23.

8. Crum, A. J., & Langer, E. (2007). Mind-set matters: Exercise and the placebo effect. *Psychological Science, 18,* 165–171.

9. Oschman, J. L., Chevalier, G., & Brown, R. (2015). The effects of grounding (earthing) on inflammation, the immune response, wound healing, and prevention and treatment of chronic inflammatory and autoimmune diseases. *Journal of Inflammation Research, 8,* 83–96. https://doi.org/10.2147/JIR.S69656.

10. Fox, N. A., & Shonkoff, J. P. (2011). How persistent fear and anxiety can affect young children's learning, behavior and health. *Early Childhood Matters* 16, 8–14.

11. Maier, S. F., & Seligman, M. E. (1976). Learned helplessness: Theory and evidence. *Journal of Experimental Psychology: General, 105,* 3–46; Maier, S. F., & Seligman, M. E. (2016). Learned helplessness at fifty: Insights from neuroscience. *Psychological Review, 123,* 349–367.

12. Bonanno, G. (2021). *The end of trauma: How the new science of resilience is changing how we think about PTSD.* New York: Basic Books.

13. Maslow, A. H. (1998; originally published in 1962). *Toward a psychology of being* (3rd ed.) New York: John Wiley & Sons, 76.

14. Schönbrodt, F. D., & Gerstenberg, F. X. R. (2012). An IRT analysis of motive questionnaires: The unified motive scales. *Journal of Research in Personality, 46*(6), 725–742.

15. Fraley, R. C., Hudson, N. W., Heffernan, M. E., & Segal, N. (2015). Are adult attachment styles categorical or dimensional? A taxometric analysis of general and relationship-specific attachment orientations. *Journal of Personality and Social Psychology, 109*(2), 354–368; Fraley, R. C., &

Spieker, S. J. (2003). Are infant attachment patterns continuously or categorically distributed? A taxometric analysis of strange situation behavior. *Developmental Psychology, 39*(3), 387–404; Mikulincer, M., & Shaver, P. R. (2016). *Attachment in adulthood: Structure, dynamics, and change* (2nd ed.). New York: Guilford Press.

16. Pinquart, M., Feussner, C., & Ahnert, L. (2013). Meta-analytic evidence for stability in attachments from infancy to early adulthood. *Attachment & Human Development, 15*(2), 189–218.

17. Simpson, J. A., & Rholes, W. S. (2017). Adult attachment, stress, and romantic relationships. *Current Opinion in Psychology, 13,* 19–24; Wiebe, S. A., & Johnson, S. M. (2017). Creating relationships that foster resilience in Emotionally Focused Therapy. *Current Opinion in Psychology, 13,* 65–69.

## Chapter 2: Connect

1. Cacioppo, J. T., & Patrick, W. (2009). *Loneliness: Human nature and the need for social connection.* New York: W. W. Norton; Joseph, S. (ed.). (2015). *Positive psychology in practice: Promoting human flourishing in work, health, education, and everyday life.* Hoboken: John Wiley & Sons.

2. Cacioppo, J. T., & Patrick, W. (2009). *Loneliness: Human nature and the need for social connection.* New York: W. W. Norton.

3. Leary, M. R., & Guadagno, J. (2011). The sociometer, self-esteem, and the regulation of interpersonal behavior. In K. D. Vohs & R. F. Baumeister (eds.), *Handbook of self-regulation: Research, theory, and applications* (pp. 339–354). New York: Guilford Press.

4. Cacioppo, J. T., et al. (2002). Do lonely days invade the nights? Potential social modulation of sleep efficiency. *Psychological Science, 13*(4), 384–387; Kurina, L. M., et al. (2011). Loneliness is associated with sleep fragmentation in a communal society. *Sleep, 34*(11), 1519–1526; Luo, Y., Hawkley, L. C., Waite, L. J., & Cacioppo, J. T. (2012). Loneliness, health, and mortality in old age: A national longitudinal study. *Social Science & Medicine, 74*(6), 907–914; Quora contributor. (2017). Loneliness might be a bigger health risk than smoking or obesity. *Forbes.* https://www.forbes.com/sites/quora/2017/01/18/loneliness-might-be-a-bigger-health-risk-than-smoking-or-obesity/amp.

5. Firger, J. (2016, April 22). Suicide rate has increased 24 percent since 1999 in the U.S., says CDC. *Newsweek.* http://www.newsweek.com/us-suicide-rates-cdc-increase-24-percent-cdc-1999-2014-451606; Routledge, C. (2018, June 23). Suicides have increased. Is there an existential crisis? *The New York Times.* https://www.nytimes.com/2018/06/23/opinion/sunday/suicide-rate-existential-crisis.html; Scelfo, J. (2015, July 27). Suicide on campus and the pressure of perfection. *The New York Times.* https://www.nytimes.com/2015/08/02/education/edlife/stress-social-media-and-suicide-on-campus.html.

6. King, R., Bialik, C., & Flowers, R. (2015, December 3). *Mass shootings have become more common in the U.S.* FiveThirtyEight. https://fivethirtyeight.com/features/mass-shootings-have-become-more-common-in-the-u-s/.

7. Leary, M. R., Kelly, K. M., Cottrell, C. A., & Schreindorfer, L. S. (2012). Construct validity of the need to belong scale: Mapping the nomological network. *Journal of Personality Assessment, 95*, 610–624.

8. Schöonbrodt, F. D., & Gerstenberg, F. X. R. (2012). An IRT analysis of motive questionnaires: The Unified Motive Scales. *Journal of Research in Personality, 46*, 725–42.

9. Mellor, D., Stokes, M., Firth, L., Hayashi, Y., & Cummins, R. (2008). Need for belonging, relationship satisfaction, loneliness, and life satisfaction. *Personality and Individual Differences, 45*, 213–218.

10. Okabe-Miyamoto, K., & Lyubomirsky, S. (2021b). *Social Connection and Well-Being during COVID-19.* https://happiness-report.s3.amazonaws.com/2021/WHR+21_Ch6.pdf.

11. Okabe-Miyamoto, K., & Lyubomirsky, S. (2021b). *Social Connection and Well-Being during COVID-19.* https://happiness-report.s3.amazonaws.com/2021/WHR+21_Ch6.pdf.

12. Fowler, J. H., & Christakis, N. A. (2008). Dynamic spread of happiness in a large social network: Longitudinal analysis over 20 years in the Framingham Heart Study. *British Medical Journal, 337*, 23–36.

13. Stephens, J. P., Heaphy, E., & Dutton, J. (2011). High quality connections. In K. Cameron and G. Spreitzer (eds.), Handbook of positive organizational scholarship (pp. 385–399). New York: Oxford University Press.

14. Dutton, J., & Heaphy, E. D. (2003). The power of high-quality connections. In K. S. Cameron, J. E. Dutton, & R. E. Quinn (eds.), *Positive organizational scholarship* (pp. 263–279). San Francisco: Berrett-Koehler Publishers, p. 264.

15. Dutton & Heaphy, The power of high-quality connections. In Cameron, Dutton, & Quinn, *Positive organizational scholarship*, p. 265.

16. Dutton & Heaphy, The power of high-quality connections. In Cameron, Dutton, & Quinn, *Positive organizational scholarship*, p. 266.

17. Rogers, C. R. (1951). *Client-centered therapy: Its current practice, implications, and theory.* Boston: Houghton-Mifflin.

18. Dutton, J. E. (2003). *Energize your workplace: How to create and sustain high-quality connections at work.* San Francisco: Jossey-Bass.

19. Cummings, L. L., & Bromiley, P. (1996). The Organizational Trust Inventory (OTI): Development and validation. In R. M. Kramer & T. R. Tyler (eds.), *Trust in organization: Frontiers of theory and research* (pp. 302–330). Thousand Oaks: Sage Publications; Diener, E., Oishi, S., & Lucas, R. E. (2003). Personality, culture, and subjective well-being: Emotional and cognitive evaluations of life. *Annual Review of Psychology, 54*, 403–425.

20. Perel, E. *Letters from Esther #22: Small talk.* Esther Perel. https://www.estherperel.com/blog/letters-from-esther-22-small-talk.

21. Aron, A., Melinat, E., Aron, E. N., Vallone, R. D., & Bator, R. J. (1997). The experimental generation of interpersonal closeness: A procedure and some preliminary findings. *Personality and Social Psychology Bulletin, 23*(4), 363–377. https://doi.org/10.1177/0146167297234003.

22. Catron, M. L. (2015, January 9). To fall in love with anyone, do this. *The New York Times*. https://www.nytimes.com/2015/01/11/style/modern-love-to-fall-in-love-with-anyone-do-this.html.

23. Langston, C. (1994). Capitalizing on and coping with daily-life events: Expressive responses to positive events. *Journal of Personality and Social Psychology, 67*, 1112–1125.

24. Gable, S. L., Reis, H. T., Impett, E. A., & Asher, E. R. (2004). What do you do when things go right? The intrapersonal and interpersonal benefits of sharing positive events. *Journal of Personality and Social Psychology, 87*, 228–245.

25. Gable, S. L., Reis, H. T., Impett, E. A., & Asher, E. R. (2004). What do you do when things go right? The intrapersonal and interpersonal benefits of sharing positive events. *Journal of Personality and Social Psychology, 87*, 228–245.

26. Kent, M., Davis, M. C., & Reich, J. W. (2014). *The resilience handbook: approaches to stress and trauma* (p. 344). New York: Routledge, Taylor & Francis Group.

27. Janoff-Bulman, R. (1979). Characterological versus behavioral self-blame: Inquiries into depression and rape. *Journal of Personality and Social Psychology, 37*, 1798–1809. https://doi.org/10.1037/0022-3514.37.10.1798.

28. Kent, M., Davis, M. C., & Reich, J. W. (2014). *The resilience handbook: approaches to stress and trauma* (p. 344). New York: Routledge, Taylor & Francis Group.

29. Wade, N. G., Bailey, D., & Shaffer, P. (2005). Helping clients heal: Does forgiveness make a difference? *Professional Psychology: Research and Practice, 36*, 634–641. https://doi.org/10.1037/0735-7028.36.6.634.

30. Berry, J. W., Worthington, E. L., Jr., Parrott, L., III, O'Connor, L. E., & Wade, N. G. (2001). Dispositional forgivingness: Development and construct validity of the Transgression Narrative Test of Forgiveness (TNTF). *Personality and Social Psychology Bulletin, 27*, 1277–1290. https://doi.org/10.1177/01461672012710004.

31. Ingersoll-Dayton, B., Campbell, R., & Hwa-Ha, J. (2011). Enhancing forgiveness: A group intervention for the elderly. *Journal of Gerontological Social Work, 52*, 2–16. https://doi.org/10.1080/01634370802561901.

32. Worthington, E. L., Jr. (2001). *Five steps to forgiveness: The art and science of forgiving*. New York: Crown House.

33. Lin, Y., Worthington, E. L., Griffin, B. J., Greer, C. L., Opare-Henaku, A., Lavelock, C. R., Hook, J. N., Ho, M. Y., & Muller, H. (2014). Efficacy of REACH forgiveness across cultures. *Journal of Clinical Psychology, 70*(9), 781–793. https://doi.org/10.1002/jclp.22073.

34. McCullough, M. E. (2000). Forgiveness as human strength: Theory, measurement, and links to well-being. *Journal of Social and Clinical Psychology, 19*(1), 43–55. https://doi.org/10.1521/jscp.2000.19.1.43; vanOyen, Witvliet, C., & Root Luna, L. (2017). Forgiveness and well-being. In *Positive psychology: established and emerging issues*. New York: Routledge.

35. Brown, R. P. (2004). Vengeance is mine: Narcissism, vengeance, and the tendency to forgive. *Journal of Research in Personality, 6*, 576–584; Fatfouta, R., Zeigler-Hill, V., & Schroder-Abe, M. (2017). I'm merciful, am I not? Facets of narcissism and forgiveness revisited. *Journal of Research in Personality, 70*, 166–173.

## Chapter 3: Develop Healthy Self-Esteem

1. Kaufman, S. B. (2017, October 29). Narcissism and self-esteem are very different. *Scientific American Blogs.* https://blogs.scientificamerican.com/beautiful-minds/narcissism-and-self-esteem-are -very-different.

2. Rosenberg, M. (1986). Self-concept from middle childhood through adolescence. In J. Suls & A. G. Greenwald (eds.), *Psychological perspectives on the self* (Vol. 3, pp. 107–135). Hillsdale: Lawrence Erlbaum Associates.

3. Items adapted from Tafarodi, R. W., & Swann, W. B., Jr. (2001). Two-dimensional self-esteem: Theory and measurement. *Personality and Individual Differences, 31*(5), 653–673.

4. Baumeister, R. F., Tice, D. M., & Hutton, D. G. (1989). Self-presentational motivations and personality differences in self-esteem. *Journal of Personality, 57*(3), 547–579, https://doi.org/10.1111/j .1467-6494.1989.tb02384.x.

5. Kaufman, S. B. (2021). *Transcend: The new science of self-actualization.* New York: TarcherPerigee; Kaufman, S. B., Weiss, B., Miller, J. D., & Campbell, W. K. (2018). Clinical correlates of vulnerable and grandiose narcissism: A personality perspective. *Journal of Personality Disorders 32,* 384.

6. Kaufman, S. B., Weiss, B., Miller, J. D., & Campbell, W. K. (2018). Clinical correlates of vulnerable and grandiose narcissism: A personality perspective. *Journal of Personality Disorders 32,* 384; Jauk, E., & Kaufman, S. B. (2018). The higher the score, the darker the core: The nonlinear association between grandiose and vulnerable narcissism. *Frontiers in Psychology,* https://doi.org/10.3389/fp -syg.2018.01305.

7. Items adapted from the following scales: Glover, N., Miller, J. D., Lynam, D. R., Crego, C., & Widiger, T. A. (2012). The Five-Factor Narcissism Inventory: A five-factor measure of narcissistic personality traits. *Journal of Personality Assessment, 94,* 500–512; Pincus, A. L., Ansell, E. B., Pimenel, C. A., Cain, N. M., Wright, A. G. C., and Levy, K. N. (2009). Initial construction and validation of the Pathological Narcissism Inventory. *Psychological Assessment, 21,* 365–379.

8. Kaufman, S. B., Weiss, B., Miller, J. D., & Campbell, W. K. (2018). Clinical correlates of vulnerable and grandiose narcissism: A personality perspective. *Journal of Personality Disorders, 32,* 384; Kaufman, S. B. (2018, September 11). Are narcissists more likely to experience impostor syndrome? *Scientific American Blogs.* https://blogs.scientificamerican.com/beautiful-minds/are-narcissists -more likely-to-experience-impostor-syndrome.

9. Neff, K. (2021). *Fierce self-compassion: How women can harness kindness to speak up, claim their power, and thrive.* New York: HarperCollins Publishers.

10. Sedikides, C. (1993). Assessment, enhancement, and verification determinants of the self-evaluation process. *Journal of Personality and Social Psychology, 65,* 317–338.

11. Aberson, C. L., Healy, M., & Romero, V. (2000). Ingroup bias and self-esteem: A meta-analysis. *Personality and Social Psychology Review, 4,* 157–173.

12. Baumeister, R. F., Smart, L., & Boden, J. M. (1996). Relation of threatened egotism to violence and aggression: The dark side of high self-esteem. *Psychological Review, 103,* 5–33.

13. Neff, K. (2021). *Fierce self-compassion: How women can harness kindness to speak up, claim their power, and thrive.* New York: HarperCollins Publishers, p. 125.

14. Gazelle, G. (2019). Personal communication.

15. Neff, K. (2021). *Fierce self-compassion: How women can harness kindness to speak up, claim their power, and thrive.* New York: HarperCollins Publishers.

16. Neff, K. (2021). *Fierce self-compassion: How women can harness kindness to speak up, claim their power, and thrive.* New York: HarperCollins Publishers.

17. Rebele, R. W. (2015). Being "otherish": Resolving the false choice between personal and prosocial goals. In R. J. Burke, K. M. Page, & C. L. Cooper (eds.), *Flourishing in life, work, and careers: Individual wellbeing and career experience* (pp. 26–44). New Horizons in Management. Cheltenham, UK: Edward Elgar Publishing.

18. Kaufman, S. B. & Jauk, E. (2020). Healthy selfishness and pathological altruism: Measuring two paradoxical forms of selfishness. *Frontiers in Psychology,* https://doi.org/10.3389/fp-syg.2020.01006.

19. Jordyn's dear friend and mentor Mike Rosenstark gave her this life-changing yet super-simple advice, which helped her think more deliberately about her priorities when her plate was very full as a medical student.

20. Paterson, R. J. (2000). *The assertiveness workbook: How to express your ideas and stand up for yourself at work and in relationships.* Oakland: New Harbinger Publications.

21. Gillihan, S. J. (2018). *Cognitive behavioral therapy made simple: 10 strategies for managing anxiety, depression, anger, panic, and worry.* Emeryville: Althea Press.

22. Burns, D. (1989). *The feeling good handbook.* New York: Morrow; Gillihan, S. J. (2018). *Cognitive behavioral therapy made simple: 10 strategies for managing anxiety, depression, anger, panic, and worry.* Emeryville: Althea Press.

23. Beck, A. T., Rush, A. J., Shaw, B. F., & Emery, G. (1979). *Cognitive therapy of depression.* New York: Guilford Press.

24. Clance, P. R. (n.d.). *Dr. Pauline Rose Clance—Impostor phenomenon.* Retrieved December 24, 2021, from https://www.paulineroseclance.com/impostor_phenomenon.html.

25. Sakulku, J., & Alexander, J. (2011). The impostor phenomenon. *International Journal of Behavioral Science, 6,* 73–92.

26. Bravata, D., Madhusudhan, D., Boroff, M., & Cokley, K. (2020). Commentary: Prevalence, predictors, and treatment of imposter syndrome: A systematic review. *Journal of Mental Health & Clinical Psychology, 4*(3), 12–16. https://doi.org/10.29245/2578-2959/2020/3.1207.

27. Chae, J.-H., Piedmont, R. L., Estadt, B. K., & Wicks, R. J. (1995). Personological evaluation of Clance's Imposter Phenomenon scale in a Korean sample. *Journal of Personality Assessment, 65*(3), 468–485. https://doi.org/10.1207/s15327752jpa6503_7; Clance, P. R., Dingman, D., Reviere, S. L., & Stober, D. R. (1995). Impostor phenomenon in an interpersonal/social context. *Women & Therapy, 16*(4), 79–96. https://doi.org/10.1300/j015v16n04_07.

28. Kaufman, S. B., Weiss, B., Miller, J. D., & Campbell, W. K. (2018). Clinical correlates of vulnerable and grandiose narcissism: A personality perspective. *Journal of Personality Disorders, 32,* 384;

Kaufman, S. B. (2018, September 11). Are narcissists more likely to experience impostor syndrome? *Scientific American Blogs.* https://blogs.scientificamerican.com/beautiful-minds/are-narcissists -more likely-to-experience-impostor-syndrome.

29. Cowman, S. E., & Ferrari, J. R. (2002). "Am I for real?" Predicting impostor tendencies from self-handicapping and affective components. *Social Behavior and Personality: An International Journal, 30*(2), 119–125; Leary, M. R., Patton, K. M., Orlando, A. E., & Funk, W. W. (2001). The impostor phenomenon: Self-perceptions, reflected appraisals, and interpersonal strategies. *Journal of Personality, 68*(4), 725–756; McElwee, R. O., & Yurak, T. J. (2007). Feeling versus acting like an impostor: Real feelings of fraudulence or self-presentation? *Individual Differences Research, 5*(3), 201–220.

30. Clance, P. R. (1986). *The impostor phenomenon when success makes you feel like a fake* (pp. 20–22). Toronto: Bantam.

31. Clance, P. R. (2017). *The impostor phenomenon: Overcoming the fear that haunts your success.* Amazon Digital Services LLC. https://www.amazon.com/Impostor-Phenomenon-Overcoming -Haunts-Success-ebook/dp/B074D3NDGQ; Thompson, T., Davis, H., & Davidson, J. (1998). Attributional and affective responses of impostors to academic success and failure outcomes. *Personality and Individual Differences, 25,* 381–396; Ferrari, J. R., & Thompson, T. (2006). Impostor fears: Links with self-perfection concerns and self-handicapping behaviours. *Personality and Individual Differences, 40,* 341–352; Thompson, T., Foreman, P., & Martin, F. (2000). Impostor fears and perfectionistic concern over mistakes. *Personality and Individual Differences, 29,* 629–647.

32. Bussotti, C. (1990). The impostor phenomenon: Family roles and environment. (Doctoral dissertation, Georgia State University). *Dissertation Abstracts International, 51,* 4041B–4042B.

33. Bussotti, C. (1990). The impostor phenomenon: Family roles and environment. (Doctoral dissertation, Georgia State University). *Dissertation Abstracts International, 51,* 4041B-4042B; Clance, P. R. (1985). *The Impostor Phenomenon: Overcoming the fear that haunts your success.* Atlanta: Peachtree Publishers; King, J. E., & Cooley, E. L. (1995). Achievement orientation and the impostor phenomenon among college students. *Contemporary Educational Psychology, 20*(3), 304–312, 1995; Sonnak, C., & Towell, T. (2001). The impostor phenomenon in British university students: Relationships between self-esteem, mental health, parental rearing style and socioeconomic status. *Personality and Individual Differences, 31*(6), 863–874.

34. Chrisman, S. M., Pieper, W. A., Clance, P. R., Holland, C. L., & Glickauf-Hughes, C. (1995). Validation of the Clance Imposter Phenomenon Scale. *Journal of Personality Assessment, 65*(3), 456–467. https://doi.org/10.1207/s15327752jpa6503_6; Henning, K., Ey, S., & Shaw, D. (1998). Perfectionism, the imposter phenomenon and psychological adjustment in medical, dental, nursing and pharmacy students. *Medical Education, 32*(5), 456–464. https://doi.org/10.1046/j.1365-2923.1998.00234.x. Topping, M. E. (1983). The impostor phenomenon: A study of its construct and incidence in university faculty members. (Doctoral dissertation, University of South Florida). *Dissertation Abstracts International, 44,* 1948B–1949B.

35. Kamarzarrin, H. (2013). A study of the relationship between self-esteem and the imposter phenomenon in the physicians of Rasht city. *European Journal of Experimental Biology, 3*(2),

363–366; Kaufman, S. B. (2021). *Transcend: The new science of self-actualization.* New York: TarcherPerigee.

36. Clance, P. R. (2017). *The impostor phenomenon: Overcoming the fear that haunts your success.* Amazon Digital Services LLC. https://www.amazon.com/Impostor-Phenomenon-Overcoming -Haunts-Success-ebook/dp/B074D3NDGQ.

37. Clance, P. R. (2017). *The impostor phenomenon: Overcoming the fear that haunts your success.* Amazon Digital Services LLC. https://www.amazon.com/Impostor-Phenomenon-Overcoming -Haunts-Success-ebook/dp/B074D3NDGQ; Sakulku, J. & Alexander, J. (2011). The impostor phenomenon. *International Journal of Behavioral Science*, 6(1), 75–97. https://doi.org/10.14456 /ijbs.2011.6.

38. Kaufman, S. B. (2021). *Transcend: The new science of self-actualization.* New York: TarcherPerigee; Maslow, A. H. (1987). *Motivation and personality* (3rd ed.). New York: HarperCollins.

39. Perfectionism graphic designed by psychiatrist Dr. Annie Hart, M.D., and Jordyn Feingold for use with medical students and patients.

## Chapter 4: Explore

1. Kashdan, T. B., & Silvia, P. J. (2011). Curiosity and interest: The benefits of thriving on novelty and challenge. In S. J. Lopez & R. Snyder (eds.), *The Oxford handbook of positive psychology* (pp. 367–374). New York: Oxford University Press.

2. Items adapted from Kashdan, T. B., et al. (2018). The five-dimensional curiosity scale: Capturing the bandwidth of curiosity and identifying four unique subgroups of curious people. *Journal of Research in Personality, 73*, 130–149.

3. Hayes, S., Wilson, K., Gifford, E., Follette, V., & Strosahl, K. (1996). Experiential avoidance and behavioral disorders: A functional dimensional approach to diagnosis and treatment. *Journal of Consulting and Clinical Psychology, 64*, 1152–1168. doi:10.1037/0022-006X.64.6.1152; Hayes, S. C. (2020). *A liberated mind: How to pivot toward what matters.* New York: Avery.

4. Coe, E., Batten, S. V., & Meyer, E. C. (2020). Chapter 19—Acceptance-based behavioral therapy for PTSD. In *Emotion in posttraumatic stress disorder* (pp. 545–566). San Diego: Academic Press; Hayes, S. C., Luoma, J. B., Bond, F. W., Masuda, A., & Lillis, J. (2006). Acceptance and commitment therapy: Model, processes, and outcomes. *Behaviour Research and Therapy, 44*, 1–25; Hayes, S. C. (2020). *A liberated mind: How to pivot toward what matters.* New York: Avery.

5. Muscara, C. (2019). *Stop missing your life: How to be deeply present in an un-present World.* New York: Hachette Books.

6. Hayes, S., Wilson, K., Gifford, E., Follette, V., & Strosahl, K. (1996). Experiential avoidance and behavioral disorders: A functional dimensional approach to diagnosis and treatment. *Journal of Consulting and Clinical Psychology, 64*, 1152–1168. doi:10.1037/0022-006X.64.6.1152.

7. May, R. (1982). The problem of evil: An open letter to Carl Rogers. *Journal of Humanistic Psychology, 22*(3), 10–21.

8. Rogers, C. R. (1961). *On becoming a person: A therapist's view of psychotherapy.* New York: Houghton Mifflin.

9. Rogers, C. R. (1961). *On becoming a person: A therapist's view of psychotherapy.* New York: Houghton Mifflin.

10. Kashdan, T., & Biswas-Diener, R. (2014). *The upside of your dark side: Why being your whole self—not just your "good" self—drives success and fulfillment.* New York: Plume.

11. Tedeschi, R., & Calhoun, L. (2004). Target article: posttraumatic growth. *Psychological Inquiry, 15,* 1–18.

12. May, R. (1969). *Love and will.* New York: W. W. Norton, pp. 129–130.

13. Vaillant, G. E. (1992). *Ego mechanisms of defense: A guide for clinicians and researchers.* Washington, DC: American Psychiatric Publishing; Vaillant, G. E. (1998). *Adaptation to life.* Cambridge: Harvard University Press.

14. Vaillant, G. E. (1998). *Adaptation to life.* Cambridge: Harvard University Press.

15. Kaplan, R. M., & Pascoe, G. C. (1977). Humorous lectures and humorous examples: Some effects upon comprehension and retention. *Journal of Educational Psychology, 69*(1), 61–65; Lomax, R. G., & Moosavi, S. A. (2002). Using humor to teach statistics: Must they be orthogonal? *Understanding Statistics, 1*(2), 113–130.

16. Gandino, G., Vesco, M., Benna, S. R., & Prastaro, M. (2010). Whiplash for the mind: Humour in therapeutic conversation. *International Journal of Psychotherapy, 14*(1), 13–24; Weaver, R. L., & Cotrell, H. W. (1987). Ten specific techniques for developing humor in the classroom. *Education, 108*(2), 167–179.

17. Dutton, J., & Heaphy, E. D. (2003). The power of high-quality connections. In K. S. Cameron, J. E. Dutton, & R. E. Quinn (eds.), *Positive organizational scholarship* (pp. 263–279). San Francisco: Berrett-Koehler Publishers; McGee, E., & Shevlin, M. (2009). Effect of humor on interpersonal attraction and mate selection. *Journal of Psychology, 143*(1), 67–77; Peterson, C., & Seligman, M. E. P. (2004). *Character strengths and virtues.* New York: Oxford University Press; Reece, B. (2014). *Putting the ha! in aha!: Humor as a tool for effective communication.* Master of Applied Positive Psychology (MAPP) Capstone Projects. 58. https://repository.upenn.edu/mapp_capstone/58/.

18. Gander, F., Proyer, R. T., Ruch, W., & Wyss, T. (2013). Strength-based positive interventions: Further evidence for their potential in enhancing well-being and alleviating depression. *Journal of Happiness Studies, 14,* 1241–1259; Proyer, R. T., Gander, F., Wellenzohn, S., & Ruch, W. (2014). Positive psychology interventions in people aged 50–79 years: Long-term effects of placebo-controlled online interventions on well-being and depression. *Aging & Mental Health, 18*(8), 997–1005. https://doi.org/10.1080/13607863.2014.899978.

19. Kaufman, S. B. (2013). Opening up openness to experience: A four-factor model and relations to creative achievement in the arts and sciences. *Journal of Creative Behavior, 47*(4), 233–255; Kaufman, S. B., et al. (2015). Openness to experience and intellect differentially predict creative achievement in the arts and sciences. *Journal of Personality, 84*(2), 248–258.

20. Kaufman, S. B., & Gregoire, C. (2016). *Wired to create: Unraveling the mysteries of the creative mind.* New York: TarcherPerigee.

21. McMillan, R. L., Kaufman, S. B., & Singer, J. L. (2013). Ode to positive constructive daydreaming. *Frontiers in Psychology, 4,* 626.

22. Torrance, E. P. (1983). The importance of falling in love with "something." *Creative Child & Adult Quarterly, 8,* 72–78.

## Chapter 5: Love

1. Vaillant, G. (2009). *Spiritual evolution: How we are wired for faith, hope, and love.* New York: Harmony Books, p. 101.

2. Salzberg, S. (2017). *Real love: The art of authentic connection.* New York: Flatiron Books.

3. Fromm, E. (1956). *The art of loving.* New York: Harper.

4. Martela & Ryan (2015). The benefits of benevolence: Basic psychological needs, beneficience, and the enhancement of well-being. *Journal of Personality, 84,* 750–764.

5. Alden, L. E., & Trew, J. L. (2013). If it makes you happy: Engaging in kind acts increases positive affect in socially anxious individuals. *Emotion, 13,* 64–75; Meier, S., & Stutzer, A. (2008). Is volunteering rewarding in itself? *Economica, 75,* 39–59; Aknin, L., Barrington-Leigh, C. P., Dunn, E. W., Helliwell, J. F., Burns, J., Biswas-Diener, R., et al. (2013). Prosocial spending and well-being: Cross-cultural evidence for a psychological universal. *Journal of Personality and Social Psychology, 104,* 635–652; Dunn, E., Aknin, L., & Norton, M. (2008). Spending money on others promotes happiness. *Science, 319,* 1687–1688; Piliavin, J. A., & Siegl, E. (2007). Health benefits of volunteering in the Wisconsin Longitudinal Study. *Journal of Health and Social Behavior, 48,* 450–464; Sheldon, K. M., Boehm, J. K., & Lyubomirsky, S. (2009). Variety is the spice of happiness: The hedonic adaptation prevention (HAP) model. In I. Boniwell & S. David (eds.), *Oxford handbook of happiness* (pp. 901–914). Oxford: Oxford University Press; Weinstein, N., & Ryan, R. M. (2010). When helping helps: Autonomous motivation for prosocial behavior and its influence on well-being for the helper and recipient. *Journal of Personality and Social Psychology, 98,* 222–244.

6. Andreoni, J. (1990). Impure altruism and donations to public goods: A theory of warm-glow giving. *Economic Journal, 100,* 464–477.

7. Aknin, L., Dunn, E. W., Sandstrom, G. M., & Norton, M. I. (2013). Does social connection turn good deeds into good feelings? On the value of putting the "social" in prosocial spending. *International Journal of Happiness and Development, 1,* 155–171; Dunn, E., Aknin, L., & Norton, M. (2008). Spending money on others promotes happiness. *Science, 319,* 1687–1688.

8. Brown, S. L., & Brown, R. M. (2006). Selective investment theory: Recasting the functional significance of close relationships. *Psychological Inquiry, 17,* 1–29; Fehr, E., & Fischbacher, U. (2003). The nature of human altruism. *Nature, 425,* 785–791; Hepach, R., Vaish, A., & Tomasello, M. (2012). Young children are intrinsically motivated to see others helped. *Psychological Science, 23,* 967–972.

9. Kaufman, S. B., Yaden, D. B., Hyde, E., & Tsukayama, E. (2019). The light vs. dark triad of person-

ality: Contrasting two very different profiles of human nature. *Frontiers in Psychology*, https://doi .org/10.3389/fpsyg.2019.00467; Neumann, C. S., Kaufman, S. B., Brinke, L., Bryce, Y., Hyde, E., & Tsukayama, E. (2020). Light and dark trait subtypes of human personality: A multi-study person-centered approach. *Personality and Individual Differences*, 164, https://doi.org/10.1016/j.paid .2020.110121.

10. Kaufman, S. B. [@sbkaufman] (2021, November 29). *In the currency of kindness, we place too much of a premium on doing and underestimate the value of being. Giving as a strategy in the service of personal gain is not the same as constantly uplifting others just by your way of being and your kind daily interactions with others* [Tweet]. Twitter. https://twitter.com/sbkaufman/status /1465484590202585094?s=20.

11. Kaufman, S. B., Yaden, D. B., Hyde, E., & Tsukayama, E. (2019). The light vs. dark triad of personality: Contrasting two very different profiles of human nature. *Frontiers in Psychology*, https://doi .org/10.3389/fpsyg.2019.00467; Neumann, C. S., Kaufman, S. B., Brinke, L., Bryce, Y., Hyde, E., & Tsukayama, E. (2020). Light and dark trait subtypes of human personality: A multi-study person-centered approach. *Personality and Individual Differences*, 164, https://doi.org/10.1016/j.paid.2020 .110121.

12. Burr, J. A., Tavares, J., & Mutchler, J. E. (2011). Volunteering and hypertension risk in later life. *Journal of Aging and Health, 23*, 24–51; Dulin, P. L., Gavala, J., Stephens, C., Kostick, M., & McDonald, J. (2012). Volunteering predicts happiness among older Māori and non-Māori in the New Zealand health, work, and retirement longitudinal study. *Aging and Mental Health, 16*, 617–624; Lyubomirsky, S., King, L., & Diener, E. (2005). The benefits of frequent positive affect: Does happiness lead to success? *Psychological Bulletin, 131*, 803–855; Musick, M. A., & Wilson, J. (2003). Volunteering and depression: The role of psychological and social resources in different age groups. *Social Science and Medicine, 56*, 259–269; Post, S. G. (2005). Altruism, happiness, and health: It's good to be good. *International Journal of Behavioral Medicine, 12*, 66–77; Wheeler, J. A., Gorey, K. M., & Greenblatt, B. (1998). The beneficial effects of volunteering for older volunteers and the people they serve: A meta-analysis. *International Journal of Aging and Human Development, 47*, 69–79; Windsor, T. D., Anstey, K. J., & Rodgers, B. (2008). Volunteering and psychological well-being among young-old adults: How much is too much? *The Gerontologist, 48*, 59–70.

13. Pressman, S. D., Kraft, T. L., & Cross, M. P. (2014). It's good to do good and receive good: The impact of a "pay it forward" style kindness intervention on giver and receiver well-being. *Journal of Positive Psychology, 10*(4), 293–302. https://doi.org/10.1080/17439760.2014.965269.

14. Datu, J. A. D., Valdez, J. P. M., McInerney, D. M., & Cayubit, R. F. (2021). The effects of gratitude and kindness on life satisfaction, positive emotions, negative emotions, and COVID-19 anxiety: An online pilot experimental study. *Applied Psychology: Health and Well-Being*, 1–15. https://doi.org /10.1111/aphw.12306.

15. Lyubomirsky, S., Sheldon, K., & Schkade, D. (2005). Pursuing happiness: The architecture of sustainable change. *Review of General Psychology, 9*, 111–131.

16. Rusbult, C. E., Finkel, E., & Kumashira, M. (2009). The Michelangelo phenomenon. *Current Directions in Psychological Science, 18*(6), 305–309.

17. Higgins, E. T. (1987). Self-discrepancy: A theory relating self and affect. *Psychological Review, 94*, 319–340.

18. Rusbult, C. E., Finkel, E., & Kumashira, M. (2009). The Michelangelo phenomenon. *Current Directions in Psychological Science, 18*(6), 305–309.

19. Kumashiro, M., Rusbult, C. E., Coolsen, M. K., Wolf, S. T., van den Bosch, M., & van der Lee, R. (2009). Partner affirmation, verification, and enhancement as determinants of attraction to potential dates: Experimental evidence of the unique effect of affirmation. Unpublished manuscript, Goldsmiths, University of London.

20. Rogers, C. (1957). The necessary and sufficient conditions of therapeutic personality change. *Journal of Consulting Psychology, 21*, 95–103. https://doi.org/10.1037/h0045357; the term unconditional positive regard was originally cited by Stanley Standal: Standal, S. (1954). *The need for positive regard: A contribution to client-centered theory*. Unpublished Ph.D. thesis, University of Chicago.

21. Brooks, A. (2019). *Love your enemies: How decent people can save America from the culture of contempt*. New York: Broadside Books, p. 81.

22. Frimer, J. , Skitka, L. J., & Motyl, M. (2017). Liberals and conservatives are similarly motivated to avoid exposure to one another's opinions. *Journal of Experimental Social Psychology, 72*, 1–12.

23. Waytz, A., Young, L. L., & Ginges, J. (2014). Motive attribution asymmetry for love vs. hate drives intractable conflict. *Proceedings of the National Academy of Sciences*, 111(44), 15687–15692. https://doi.org/10.1073/pnas.1414146111.

24. Aron, A., Melinat, E., Aron, E. N., Vallone, R. D., & Bator, R. J. (1997). The experimental generation of interpersonal closeness: A procedure and some preliminary findings. *Personality and Social Psychology Bulletin*, 23(4), 363–377. https://doi.org/10.1177/0146167297234003.

25. Boothby, E. J., & Bohns, V. K. (2020). Why a simple act of kindness is not as simple as it seems: Underestimating the positive impact of our compliments on others. *Personality and Social Psychology Bulletin*. https://doi.org/10.1177/0146167220949003.

26. Algoe, S. B., Dwyer, P. C., Younge, A., & Oveis, C. (2020). A new perspective on the social functions of emotions: Gratitude and the witnessing effect. *Journal of Personality and Social Psychology, 119*, 40–74, https://doi.org/10.1037/pspi0000202; Brooks, A. C. (2015, November 21). Opinion: Choose to be grateful. It will make you happier. *The New York Times*. https://www.nytimes.com/2015/11/22/opinion/sunday/choose-to-be-grateful-it-will-make-you-happier.html.

## Chapter 6: Harness Your Strengths

1. Linley, P. A., & Harrington, S. (2006). Strengths coaching: A potential-guided approach to coaching psychology. *International Coaching Psychology Review, 1*(1), 37–46.

2. Niemiec, R. M. (2014). *Mindfulness and character strengths: a practical guide to flourishing*. Boston: Hogrefe.

3. Biswas-Diener, R. (2003). From the equator to the North Pole: A study of character strengths. *Journal of Happiness Studies, 7,* 293–310; Niemiec, R. M. (2013). VIA character strengths: Research and practice (The first 10 years). In H. H. Knoop & A. Delle Fave (eds.), *Well-being and cultures: Perspectives on positive psychology* (pp. 11–30). New York: Springer.

4. Peterson, C., & Seligman, M. E. P. (2004). *Character strengths and virtues: A handbook and classification.* Washington, DC: American Psychological Association Press and Oxford University Press.

5. Niemiec, R. M. (2014). *Mindfulness and character strengths: a practical guide to flourishing.* Boston: Hofgrefe. Copyright 2004–2022 VIA Institute on Character. All rights reserved. Used with permission. www.viacharacter.org.

6. Peterson, C., & Seligman, M. E. P. (2004). *Character strengths and virtues: A handbook and classification.* Washington, DC: American Psychological Association Press and Oxford University Press.

7. Biswas-Diener, R., Kashdan, T. B., & Minhas, G. (2011). A dynamic approach to psychological strength development and intervention. *Journal of Positive Psychology, 6*(2), 106–118.

8. Niemiec, R. M. (2014). *Mindfulness and character strengths: a practical guide to flourishing.* Boston: Hogrefe.

9. Niemiec, R. M. (2014). *Mindfulness and character strengths: a practical guide to flourishing* (pp. 28–29). Boston: Hogrefe.

10. *About Character Lab.* (n.d.). Character Lab. Retrieved December 24, 2021, from https://characterlab.org/about/.

11. Linley, A. (2008). *Average to A+: Realising strengths in yourself and others.* Coventry, UK: CAPP Press.

12. Niemiec, R. M. (2014). *Mindfulness and character strengths: a practical guide to flourishing* (p. 89). Boston: Hogrefe.

13. Niemiec, R. M. (2019). Finding the golden mean: the overuse, underuse, and optimal use of character strengths. *Counselling Psychology Quarterly,* https://doi.org/10.1080/09515070.2019.1617674.

14. *Mindfulness-Based Strengths Practice Certification, VIA Institute.* (n.d.). Retrieved December 25, 2021, from https://www.viacharacter.org/courses/mindfulness-based-strength-practice-certification.

15. This approach and these questions are all adapted from Niemiec's *Mindfulness and character strengths.*

16. Seligman, M. E. P., Steen, T. A., Park, N., & Peterson, C. (2005). Positive psychology progress: Empirical validation of interventions. *American Psychologist, 60*(5), 410–421. https://doi.org/10.1037/0003-066x.60.5.410.

17. Schwartz, B., & Sharpe, K. E. (2006). Practical wisdom: Aristotle meets positive psychology. *Journal of Happiness Studies, 7,* 377–395.

18. Niemiec, R. (2012, April 19). *Tips for using each character strength in a new way.* VIA Institute. https://www.viacharacter.org/topics/articles/tips-for-using-each-character-strength-in-a-new-way.

## Chapter 7: Live Your Purpose

1. Maslow, A. H. (1965). *Eupsychian management: A journal*. Homewood: Richard D. Irwin, Inc., and the Dorsey Press, p. 6.

2. Edge. (2016, March 16). *The mattering instinct: A conversation with Rebecca Newberger Goldstein*. Edge. https://www.edge.org/conversation/rebecca_newberger_goldstein-the-mattering-instinct.

3. Bugental, J. F. T. (1965). *The search for authenticity: An existential-analytic approach to psychotherapy*. New York: Holt, Rinehart and Winston, pp. 267–272; Kaufman, S. B. (2021). *Transcend: The new science of self-actualization*. New York: TarcherPerigee.

4. Esfahani Smith, E. (2017, September 4). You'll never be famous—and that's O.K. *The New York Times*. https://www.nytimes.com/2017/09/04/opinion/middlemarch-college-fame.html.

5. Wrzesniewski, A., McCauley, C., Rozin, P., & Schwartz, B. (1997). Jobs, careers, and callings: People's relations to their work. *Journal of Research in Personality, 31*(1), 21–33.

6. Maslow, A. H. (1965). *Eupsychian management: A journal*. Homewood: Richard D. Irwin, Inc., and the Dorsey Press.

7. Note: Connecting with the meaning inherent in the work that we do and creating new explicit meanings does not absolve unhealthy or even toxic workplaces from being accountable to serving employees' rights to workplace well-being.

8. Berg, J. M., Dutton, J. E., & Wrzesniewski, A. (2013). Job crafting and meaningful work. In B. J. Dik, Z. S. Byrne, & M. F. Steger (eds.), *Purpose and meaning in the workplace* (pp. 81–104). Washington, DC: American Psychological Association.

9. Schwartz, S. H. (2012). An overview of the Schwartz theory of basic values. *Online Readings in Psychology and Culture, 2*, 1. http://dx.doi.org/10.9707/2307-0919.1116.

10. Schwartz, S. H., Cieciuch, J., Vecchione, M., Davidov, E., Fischer, R., Beierlein, C., Ramos, A., Verkasalo, M., Lönnqvist, J.-E., Demirutku, K., Dirilen-Gumus, O., & Konty, M. (2012). Refining the theory of basic individual values. *Journal of Personality and Social Psychology, 103*(4), 663–688. https://doi.org/10.1037/a0029393.

11. Schwartz, S. (2017). The refined theory of basic values. In S. Roccas & L. Sagiv (eds.), *Values and behavior: Taking a cross-cultural perspective*. Cham, Switzerland: Springer 163–228. https://doi.org/10.1007/978-3-319-56352-7_3; Cieciuch, J., Davidov, E., Vecchione, M., Beierlein, C., & Schwartz, S. H. (2014). The cross-national invariance properties of a new scale to measure 19 basic human values: A test across eight countries. *Journal of Cross-Cultural Psychology, 45*(5), 764–776.

12. https://www.facebook.com/BlueZones. (2015). How to live longer, better: Discovering the Blue Zones. Blue Zones. https://www.bluezones.com/live-longer-better/.

13. Fido, D., Kotera, Y., & Asano, K. (2019). English translation and validation of the Ikigai-9 in a UK sample. *International Journal of Mental Health and Addiction, 18*, 1352–1359.

14. Fido, D., Kotera, Y., & Asano, K. (2019). English translation and validation of the Ikigai-9 in a UK sample. *International Journal of Mental Health and Addiction, 18*, 1352–1359.

15. Many of these questions are adapted from Jeremy Sutton's article: Sutton, J. (2021, February 15). 6

*worksheets & templates to find your ikigai*. PositivePsychology.com. https://positivepsychology .com/ikigai-worksheets-templates/.

16. Esfahani Smith, E. (2021, June 24). Opinion: We want to travel and party. Hold that thought. *The New York Times*. https://www.nytimes.com/2021/06/24/opinion/covid-pandemic-grief.html.

17. Esfahani Smith, E. (2021, June 24). Opinion: We want to travel and party. Hold that thought. *The New York Times*. https://www.nytimes.com/2021/06/24/opinion/covid-pandemic-grief.html.

18. Yalom, I. D. (1980). *Existential psychotherapy*. New York: Basic Books, p. 31.

19. Vail, K. E., Juhl, J., Arndt, J., Vess, M., Routledge, C., & Rutjens, B. (2012). When death is good for life: Considering the positive trajectories of terror management. *Personality and Social Psychology Review, 16*(4), 303–329.

20. Cozzolino, P. J., Blackie, L. E. R., & Meyers, L. S. (2014). Self-related consequences of death fear and death denial. *Death Studies, 38*(6), 418–422; Lykins, E. L., Segerstrom, S. C., Averill, A. J., Evans, D. R., & Kemeny, M. E. (2007). Goal shifts following reminders of mortality: Reconciling posttraumatic growth and terror management theory. *Personality and Social Psychology Bulletin, 33*(8), 1088–1099.

21. Yalom, I. D. (1980). *Existential psychotherapy*. New York: Basic Books.

**Chapter 8: Become a Transcender**

1. Maslow, A. H. (1993/1971). *The farther reaches of human nature*. New York: Penguin Books.

2. Kabat-Zinn, J. (2005). *Wherever you go, there you are: Mindfulness meditation in everyday life*. New York: Hachette Books.

3. Kaufman, S. B. (2011, January 11). The science of spiritual narcissism. *Scientific American*. https:// www.scientificamerican.com/article/the-science-of-spiritual-narcissism/.

4. Kaufman, S. B. (2021). *Transcend: The new science of self-actualization*. New York: Tarcher-Perigee.

5. Maslow, A. H. (1969). The farther reaches of human nature. *Journal of Transpersonal Psychology, 1*(1), 1–9, p. 1. The entire lecture at the Unitarian church can be found on YouTube at https://www .youtube.com/watch?v=pagvjnTEEvg.

6. Kaufman, S. B. (2021). *Transcend: The new science of self-actualization*. New York: TarcherPerigee.

7. Maslow, A. H. (1993/1971). *The farther reaches of human nature*. New York: Penguin Books.

8. Maslow, A. H. (1993/1971). *The farther reaches of human nature*. New York: Penguin Books.

9. Wong, P. (2020, October 5). *Existential positive psychology (PP 2.0) and the new science of flourishing through suffering*. Dr. Paul T Wong. http://www.drpaulwong.com/existential-positive -psychology-pp-2-0-and-the-new-science-of-flourishing-through-suffering/.

10. Bryant, F. B., & Veroff, J. (2007). *Savoring: A new model of positive experience*. Mahwah: Lawrence Erlbaum Associates, Inc. https://doi.org/10.1080/17439760701794434.

11. Bryant, F. B., & Veroff, J. (2007). *Savoring: A new model of positive experience*. Mahwah: Lawrence Erlbaum Associates, Inc. https://doi.org/10.1080/17439760701794434.

12. Hou, W. K., Lau, K. M., Ng, S. M., Lee, T. M., Cheung, H. Y., Shum, T. C., et al. (2016). Psychological detachment and savoring in adaptation to cancer caregiving. *Psycho-Oncology, 25*(7), 839–847. https://doi.org/10.1002/pon.4065; Hurley, D. B., & Kwon, P. (2012). Results of a study to increase savoring the moment: Differential impact on positive and negative outcomes. *Journal of Happiness Studies, 13*(4), 579–588. https://doi.org/10.1007/s10902-011-9280-8; Jose, P. E., Lim, B. T., Kim, S., & Bryant, F. B. (2018). Does savoring mediate the relationship between explanatory style and mood outcomes? *Journal of Positive Psychology and Well-being, 2*(2), 149–167; McMakin, D. L., Siegle, G. J., & Shirk, S. R. (2011). Positive affect stimulation and sustainment (PASS) module for depressed mood: A preliminary investigation of treatment-related effects. *Cognitive Therapy Research, 35*(3), 217–226; Ng, W. (2012). Neuroticism and well-being? Let's work on the positive rather than negative aspects. *Journal of Positive Psychology, 7*(5), 416–426. https://doi.org/10.1080/17439760.2012.709270.

13. Costa-Ramalho, S., Marques-Pinto, A., Ribeiro, M. T., & Pereira, C. R. (2015). Savoring positive events in couple life: Impacts on relationship and dyadic adjustment. *Family Science, 6*(1), 170–180.

14. Burkhart, M. L., Borelli, J. L., Rasmussen, H. F., & Sbarra, D. A. (2015). Cherish the good times: Relational savoring in parents of infants and toddlers. *Personal Relationships, 22*(4), 692–711.

15. Sato, I., Conner, T. S., & Jose, P. E. (2017). Savoring mediates the effect of nature on positive affect. *International Journal of Well-being, 8*(1), 18–33.

16. Garland, E. L., Thielking, P., Thomas, E. A., Coombs, M., White, S., Lombardi, J., et al. (2016). Linking dispositional mindfulness and positive psychological processes in cancer survivorship: A multivariate path analytic test of the mindfulness-to-meaning theory. *Psycho-Oncology.* https://doi.org/10.1002/pon.4065; Otto, A. K., Laurenceau, J. P., Siegel, S. D., & Belcher, A. J. (2015). Capitalizing on everyday positive events uniquely predicts daily intimacy and well-being in couples coping with breast cancer. *Journal of Family Psychology, 29*(1), 69–79. https://doi.org/10.1037/fam0000042.

17. Jose, P. E., Lim, B. T., Kim, S., & Bryant, F. B. (2018). Does savoring mediate the relationship between explanatory style and mood outcomes? *Journal of Positive Psychology and Well-being, 2*(2), 149–167.

18. Smith, J. L., & Hollinger-Smith, L. (2015). Savoring, resilience, and psychological well-being in older adults. *Aging & Mental Health, 19*(3), 192–200.

19. Bryant, F. B. (2003). Savoring beliefs inventory (SBI): A scale for measuring beliefs about savoring. *Journal of Mental Health, 12*(2), 175–196.

20. Bryant, F. B., & Veroff, J. (2007). *Savoring: A new model of positive experience.* Mahwah: Lawrence Erlbaum Associates, Inc. https://doi.org/10.1080/17439760701794434.

21. Bryant, F. B. (2003). Savoring beliefs inventory (SBI): A scale for measuring beliefs about savoring. *Journal of Mental Health, 12*(2), 175–196.

22. Bryant, F. B., & Veroff, J. (2007). *Savoring: A new model of positive experience.* Mahwah: Lawrence Erlbaum Associates, Inc. https://doi.org/10.1080/17439760701794434.

23. Bryant, F. B., & Veroff, J. (2007). *Savoring: A new model of positive experience.* Mahwah: Lawrence Erlbaum Associates, Inc. https://doi.org/10.1080/17439760701794434.

24. Smith, J. L., Harrison, P. R., Kurtz, J. L., & Bryant, F. B. (2014). Nurturing the capacity to savor: Interventions to enhance the enjoyment of positive experiences. In A. C. Parks & S. M. Schueller (eds.), *The Wiley Blackwell handbook of positive psychological interventions* (p. 42). West Sussex, UK: John Wiley & Sons.

25. Brown, B. (2021, March 8). *Brené with Dr. Susan David on the dangers of toxic positivity, Part 1 of 2*. Brené Brown. https://brenebrown.com/podcast/brene-with-dr-susan-david-on-the-dangers -of-toxic-positivity-part-1-of-2/; Brown, B. (2021, March 8). *Brené with Dr. Susan David on the dangers of toxic positivity, Part 2 of 2*. Brené Brown. https://brenebrown.com/podcast/brene-with -dr-susan-david-on-the-dangers-of-toxic-positivity-part-2-of-2/; Goodman, W. (2022). *Toxic positivity: Keeping it real in a world obsessed with being happy*. New York: TarcherPerigee; Kaufman, S. B. (2021, August 18). The opposite of toxic positivity. *The Atlantic*. https://www.theatlantic.com/family /archive/2021/08/tragic-optimism-opposite-toxic-positivity/619786/.

26. Emmons, R. (2013, May 13). How gratitude can help you through hard times. *Greater Good*. https:// greatergood.berkeley.edu/article/item/how_gratitude_can_help_you_through_hard_times.

27. Frankl, V. (1984). Postscript: The case for a tragic optimism. In *Man's Search for Meaning*. New York: Simon & Schuster; Wong, P. T. P. (n.d.). *Viktor Frankl: Prophet of hope and herald of positive psychology: International network on personal meaning*. International Network on Personal Meaning. Retrieved December 25, 2021, from https://www.meaning.ca/article/viktor-frankl-prophet-hope -herald-positive-psychology/.

28. Emmons, R. A., & Stern, R. (2013). Gratitude as a psychotherapeutic intervention. *Journal of Clinical Psychology, 69*(8), 846–855. https://doi.org/10.1002/jclp.22020.

29. Emmons, R. A., & Stern, R. (2013). Gratitude as a psychotherapeutic intervention. *Journal of Clinical Psychology, 69*(8), 846–855. https://doi.org/10.1002/jclp.22020.

30. Emmons, B. (2008). *Thanks!: How practicing gratitude can make you happier*. New York: Mariner Books.

31. Taylor, Shelley. (1983). Adjustment to threatening events—A theory of cognitive adaptation. *American Psychologist, 38*, 1161–1173. 10.1037/0003-066X.38.11.1161.; Emmons, R. A. (2007). *Thanks!: How the new science of gratitude can make you happier*. New York: Houghton Mifflin.

32. Kripalu Center for Yoga & Health (2019, October 10). *Ten true things about gratefulness: A conversation with Kristi Nelson*. Gratefulness.org. https://gratefulness.org/blog/ten-true-things-about -gratefulness-a-conversation-with-kristi-nelson/.

33. Rosmarin, D. H., Krumrei, E. J., & Pargament, K. I. (2010). Are gratitude and spirituality protective factors against psychopathology? *International Journal of Existential Psychology, 3*(1).

34. Nelson, K. (n.d.). *It's all about the glass*. Gratefulness.org. https://gratefulness.org/resource/its -all-about-the-glass/.

35. Jans-Beken, L., & Wong, P. T. P. (2019). Development and preliminary validation of the Existential Gratitude Scale (EGS). *Counselling Psychology Quarterly*, 1–15. https://doi.org/10.1080/09515070 .2019.1656054.

36. Yalom, I. D. (1980). *Existential psychotherapy*. New York: Basic Books.

37. Solom, R., Watkins, P. C., McCurrach, D., & Scheibe, D. (2016). Thieves of thankfulness: Traits that inhibit gratitude. *Journal of Positive Psychology, 12*(2), 120–129. https://doi.org/10.1080/17439760.2016.1163408.

38. Cozzolino, P. J., Staples, A. D., Meyers, L. S., & Samboceti, J. (2004). Greed, death, and values: From terror management to transcendence management theory. *Society for Personality and Social Psychology, 30,* 278–292.

39. Frias, A., Watkins, P., Webber, A., & Froh, J. (2011). Death and gratitude: Death reflection enhances gratitude. *Journal of Positive Psychology, 6,* 154–162. https://doi.org/10.1080/17439760.2011.558848.

40. Kripalu Center for Yoga & Health (2019, October 10). *Ten true things about gratefulness: A conversation with Kristi Nelson.* Gratefulness.org. https://gratefulness.org/blog/ten-true-things-about-gratefulness-a-conversation-with-kristi-nelson/.

41. Kripalu Center for Yoga & Health (2019, October 10). *Ten true things about gratefulness: A conversation with Kristi Nelson.* Gratefulness.org. https://gratefulness.org/blog/ten-true-things-about-gratefulness-a-conversation-with-kristi-nelson/.

42. Csíkszentmihály, M. (1990). *Flow: The psychology of optimal experience,* New York: Harper & Row; Kotler, S. (2014). *The rise of superman: Decoding the science of ultimate human performance.* New York: Houghton Mifflin Harcourt.

43. Csíkszentmihály, M. (1990). *Flow: The psychology of optimal experience.* New York: Harper & Row.

44. Lyubomirsky, S. (2008). *The how of happiness: A scientific approach to getting the life you want.* New York: Penguin Press.

45. As cited in Kaufman, S. B. (2021). *Transcend: The new science of self-actualization.* New York: TarcherPerigee.

46. Keltner, D., & Haidt, J. (2003). Approaching awe, a moral, spiritual, and aesthetic emotion. *Cognition & Emotion, 17*(2), 297–314. https://doi.org/10.1080/02699930302297; Yaden, D. B., Kaufman, S. B., Hyde, E., Chirico, A., Gaggioli, A., Wei Zhang, J., & Keltner, D. (2018). The development of the Awe Experience Scale (AWE-S): A multifactorial measure for a complex emotion. *Journal of Positive Psychology, 14*(4), 474–488.

47. Krause, N., & Hayward, R. D. (2015). Assessing whether practical wisdom and awe of God are associated with life satisfaction. *Psychology of Religion and Spirituality, 7*(1), 51–59. https://doi.org/10.1037/a0037694.

48. Rudd, M., Vohs, K. D., & Aaker, J. (2012). Awe expands people's perception of time, alters decision making, and enhances well-being. *Psychological Science, 23*(10), 1130–1136. https://doi.org/10.1177/0956797612438731.

49. Prade, C., & Saroglou, V. (2016). Awe's effects on generosity and helping. *Journal of Positive Psychology, 11*(5), 522–530. https://doi.org/10.1080/17439760.2015.1127992.

50. Yang, Y., Yang, Z., Bao, T., Liu, Y., & Passmore, H.-A. (2016). Elicited awe decreases aggression. *Journal of Pacific Rim Psychology, 10.* https://doi.org/10.1017/prp.2016.8.

51. Kramer, D. A. (2000). Wisdom as a classical source of human strength: Conceptualization and empirical inquiry. *Journal of Social and Clinical Psychology, 19*(1), 83–101.

52. One of our favorite books on the topic of this improv technique is by Kelly Leonard: Leonard, K. (2015). *Yes, and: How improvisation reverses "no, but" thinking and improves creativity and collaboration—lessons from the Second City.* New York: Harper Business.

53. Elam, B. (2020). *"Yes and": Exploring and heightening the positive psychology in improvisation.* Master of Applied Positive Psychology (MAPP) Capstone Projects. 188. https://repository.upenn.edu/mapp_capstone/188/.

54. Elam, B. (2020). *"Yes and": Exploring and heightening the positive psychology in improvisation* (p. 17). Master of Applied Positive Psychology (MAPP) Capstone Projects. 188. https://repository.upenn.edu/mapp_capstone/188/.

## Conclusion: Community Actualization

1. Prilleltensky, I., & Prilleltensky, O. (2021). *How people matter: Why it affects health, happiness, love, work, and society.* Cambridge: Cambridge University Press, p. 6.

2. Prilleltensky, I., & Prilleltensky, O. (2021). *How people matter: Why it affects health, happiness, love, work, and society.* Cambridge: Cambridge University Press, p. 6; Prilleltensky, I. (2021, September 16). *Freedom and community: Holding the tension.* Professor Isaac Prilleltensky. https://www.professorisaac.com/mattering/holdthetension.

3. Prilleltensky, I. (2021, September 16). *Freedom and community: Holding the tension.* Professor Isaac Prilleltensky. https://www.professorisaac.com/mattering/holdthetension.

4. Kaufman, S. B. (2021, November 6). What collective narcissism does to society. *The Atlantic.* https://www.theatlantic.com/family/archive/2021/11/group-narcissism/620632/.

5. Prilleltensky, I., & Prilleltensky, O. (2021). *How people matter: Why it affects health, happiness, love, work, and society* (p. 6). Cambridge: Cambridge University Press.

6. Katz, R. (2018). *Indigenous healing psychology: Honoring the wisdom of the first peoples.* Rochester, VT: Healing Arts; Kaufman, S. B. (2019). Honoring the wisdom of indigenous people with Richard Katz. *The Psychology Podcast.* https://scottbarrykaufman.com/podcast/honoring-the-wisdom-of-indigenous-peoples-with-richard-katz.

7. Blackstock, C. (2011). The emergence of the breath of life theory. *Journal of Social Work Values and Ethics,* 8(1); Ravilochan, T. (2021, April 4). *Could the Blackfoot wisdom that inspired Maslow guide us now?* Medium. https://gatherfor.medium.com/maslow-got-it-wrong-ae45d6217a8c; Kaufman, S. B. (2021). *Transcend: The new science of self-actualization.* New York: TarcherPerigee; Michel, K. L. (2014). Maslow's hierarchy connected to Blackfoot beliefs. *A Digital Native American.* https://lincolnmichel.wordpress.com/2014/04/19/maslows-hierarchy-connected-to-blackfoot-beliefs.

8. Coon, D. (2006). Abraham H. Maslow: Reconnaissance for eupsycia. In D. A. Dewsbury, L. T. Benjamin, Jr., & M. Wertheimer (eds.). *Portraits of Pioneers in Psychology,* Vol. 6 (pp. 255–273). Washington, DC, and Mahwah: American Psychological Association and Lawrence Erlbaum Associates.

# NOTES

9. Ravilochan, T. (2021, April 4). *Could the Blackfoot wisdom that inspired Maslow guide us now?* Medium. https://gatherfor.medium.com/maslow-got-it-wrong-ae45d6217a8c.

10. Blackstock, C. (2011). The emergence of the breath of life theory. *Journal of Social Work Values and Ethics, 8*(1).

11. Blackstock, C. (2011). The emergence of the breath of life theory. *Journal of Social Work Values and Ethics, 8*(1).

12. Ravilochan, T. (2021, April 4). *Could the Blackfoot wisdom that inspired Maslow guide us now?* Medium. https://gatherfor.medium.com/maslow-got-it-wrong-ae45d6217a8c.

# ABOUT THE AUTHORS

**Scott Barry Kaufman, PhD,** is a cognitive scientist and humanistic psychologist exploring the depths of human potential. He is a professor at Columbia University and founder and director of the Center for Human Potential. He is the author/editor of ten books, including *Choose Growth, Transcend: The New Science of Self-Actualization, Wired to Create: Unraveling the Mysteries of the Creative Mind* (with Carolyn Gregoire), and *Ungifted: Intelligence Redefined.* He is also the host of *The Psychology Podcast,* which has received more than twenty million downloads. Dr. Kaufman received a PhD in cognitive psychology from Yale University and has taught courses on intelligence, cognitive science, creativity, and well-being at Columbia University, Yale, New York University, the University of Pennsylvania, and elsewhere. In 2015, he was named one of "50 Groundbreaking Scientists Who Are Changing the Way We See the World" by *Business Insider.*

**Jordyn H. Feingold, MD, MAPP, MSCR,** is a resident physician in psychiatry at the Icahn School of Medicine at Mount Sinai in New York City, a well-being researcher, and a positive psychology practitioner, working to bring the science of self-actualization and transcendence to clinicians and patients everywhere. She graduated from the University of Pennsylvania with her BA and Master of Applied Positive Psychology (MAPP) and graduated from the Icahn School of Medicine at Mount Sinai with her MD and master's of science in clinical research (MSCR). Her research and clinical interests involve disorders of gut-brain interaction and the biopsychosocial model of digestive disorders, healthcare worker and patient well-being, and incorporating positive psychology approaches into healthcare delivery. She is involved in research, curriculum development, teaching, and advocacy locally and nationally on these topics, and is a founder of the emerging field of positive medicine. She has developed and teaches an elective course called Positive Medicine at Mount Sinai and is cofounder of the trainee well-being curriculum called PEERS: Practice Enhancement, Engagement, Resilience, and Support. She is deeply honored to have coauthored *Choose Growth,* her first book.

Also by

## Scott Barry Kaufman, PhD

"This is the book we've all been waiting for—nothing less than
a breathtaking new psychology of humanity."
—SUSAN CAIN, *New York Times* bestselling author of *Quiet*

# TRANSCEND

## THE NEW SCIENCE OF
## SELF-ACTUALIZATION

### Scott Barry Kaufman, Ph.D.

Host of *The Psychology Podcast*

tp
tarcher
perigee